HAUNTED
LAS VEGAS

Other Books in Pelican's Haunted America Series

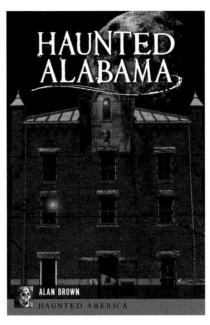

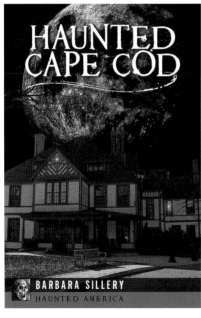

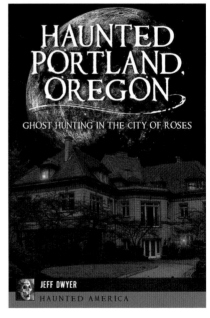

HAUNTED LAS VEGAS

JANICE OBERDING

Haunted America

PELICAN PUBLISHING
NEW ORLEANS 2021

The word "Pelican" and the depiction of a pelican
are trademarks of Arcadia Publishing Company Inc.
and are registered in the U.S. Patent and Trademark Office.

ISBN 9781455626465
Ebook ISBN 9781455626472

Printed in the United States of America
Published by Pelican Publishing
New Orleans, LA
www.pelicanpub.com

*To my husband, Bill, for the years
of love and understanding*

Contents

Chapter 1: Hauntspitality   11

Chapter 2: Public Places and Phantom Faces   31

Chapter 3: That's Show Biz   49

Chapter 4: Guns and Ghosts   71

Chapter 5: Las Vegas Early Days   95

Chapter 6: Bureaucracy, Red Tape,
  and Specters   113

Chapter 7: Boulder City Haunts   123

Chapter 8: Ghosts of Goodsprings   137

Chapter 9: Lost City, Valley of Fire,
  Logandale, and Lake Mead   147

Chapter 10: Entrepreneurial Spirits   161

Bibliography   175

HAUNTED
LAS VEGAS

Chapter 1

Hauntspitality

Welcome to Las Vegas; a city in continual flux. Developers with deep pockets discover the valley and build fabulous hotels that are remodeled, renamed, and imploded, so that other developers with even deeper pockets can start the process all over again. All the while the neon never dims, and the doors never close. So when does the city sleep? It doesn't. And that round-the-clock action, coupled with a toasty desert climate (more than three hundred days of sunshine each year) has helped to make Las Vegas one of the world's top tourist destinations. Each year millions of visitors come to the city seeking its special brand of excitement not found anywhere else. In this atmosphere of 24/7 pleasure, some overindulge and burn the candle at both ends. Eventually though, even the hardiest of souls needs some rest.

Before You Check In . . .

The hotel industry in Las Vegas, AKA Sin City, strives to make its visitors feel welcome; this is in the hope that visitors will spend hours, and dollars, at the slot machines, the roulette wheels, and the card tables. Yes, there is world-class shopping, entertainment, and dining here, but it is gambling that built this metropolis of a million-plus denizens.

Behind their outward facades, large resort hotel/casinos are arranged similarly. Row after row after row of slot machines frame the pit where the card tables and the roulette wheel are located; farthest from the action is usually the keno game. What distinguishes one establishment from the next are its décor and theme, giving each its own unique ambiance and charm. Charming as they may be, hotel/casinos fiercely compete to keep customers loyal to their particular property. The magic word here is "comp." The more you spend, the better your comp.

Never forget that this is a quid pro quo sorta city; the person who spends the most receives the most. It's logical. The whale (Las Vegas lingo for someone who drops more money in the casino annually than most people earn in a decade) will get the most lavish comp package of all. Nothing is too good for the gambler who isn't afraid to let the dice, and the good times, roll. Round-the-clock gourmet meals, a penthouse suite, a Jacuzzi hot tub the size of most hotel rooms, champagne (no cheap stuff) in a silver ice bucket, orchids, roses, chocolates, and high-definition TVs that cover the walls—all part of the we-love-ya treatment.

Coming back down to earth, the loyal low-budget gambler is also comped, but not nearly so regally: a free meal here and there, a show ticket or room on occasion. The gambler with less money to burn usually has to ask for any comps. Just remember not to ask if you aren't dropping a steady stream of dollars. This way you won't be too disappointed when management politely declines, because it will. Don't take it personally. It's all about the bottom line.

In Vegas the room choices are limitless. Whether you choose to stay in a lavish resort hotel on that two-and-a-half-mile length of Las Vegas Boulevard known as "The Strip," or a more pocketbook-friendly motel nearer the airport, you just might have a brush with the supernatural side. It's no secret that many of Las Vegas's hotels and motels have a ghost or two in residence, guests who have checked in and never checked out. You may not find mention of them in any of the Las Vegas Convention and Visitors Authority's slick magazine and television ad campaigns. But they are here nonetheless.

Bally's Las Vegas

Most paranormal experts agree that ghostly activity is often the result of great tragedy and sudden, unexpected loss of life. The MGM Grand Hotel fire early on the morning of November 21, 1980, was certainly such an event. Built in 1973 the MGM Grand Hotel Casino was ultramodern and up to the minute. Towering over many of the other hotels in the city, the twenty-six-story hotel at 3645 Las Vegas Boulevard was to be the signal of a new era dawning in Las Vegas, an era of even more change and excitement than that of the previous decade. Instead, it became the site of the worst disaster in Nevada's history, and one of the worst hotel fires in the world.

Thanksgiving was six days away. In other climes, December's bitter cold was fast approaching; in Las Vegas the weather was typical, warm and mild. The city was swarming with tourists. Comdek, the large electronic convention, was in town for its annual preview of all things new and exciting in the electronic industry. Business was brisk throughout the city. The MGM Grand was booked at 99 percent capacity, due in part to Comdek and the popular Mac Davis Show that was being featured in the fabulous nine-hundred-seat Celebrity Room.

While many of the hotel's guests slept, faulty wiring ignited a fire in the wall of the ground-floor deli. Two employees tried to contain the fire and failed. The horror was set in motion. It was already too late to avert the fire's destruction. Within minutes the fast-moving flames fanned out and spread through the casino floor. Plastic molding, carpeting, wallpaper, and other such combustible materials used in the hotel's construction quickly ignited and melted in the fire's wake, releasing toxic fumes into the air. There was no time to think, no time to run. People working and gambling in the ground-floor casino were overcome by the fumes and died where they stood.

Many tower guests were unaware of the danger until it was

too late. As flames engulfed the ground floor, shooting upward, thick black smoke rose up through the building's heating and air conditioning system. Alerted by several helicopters hovering around the building, and the unmistakable smell of the spreading flames, guests started dialing the hotel front desk. There was nothing left of that area. Phone lines were dead. Panic stricken, the anxious guests turned on their televisions and realized what was happening.

Reactions were swift. Calmly placing wet towels over their faces, a number of guests awaited rescue that would not come in time to save them. Others were doomed when they rushed out into hallways and opened stairwell doors. Frightened and disoriented, one person leaped from the north side of the tower to the parking lot far below. A lucky few would manage to escape death by making their way through the blinding smoke and noxious fumes to the rooftop where firemen and rescuers had stacked bodies for transport on helicopters that hovered noisily overhead. The dead were taken to the parking lot for further identification; the injured were transported to local hospitals. It would take another four hours for the building to be evacuated.

Of the more than five thousand people in the MGM Grand Hotel on the morning of November 21, 1980, six hundred and fifty were injured enough to seek medical attention. Eighty-seven perished in the fire.

Months passed. The lengthy investigations were completed; the charred rubble was cleared away. And the lawsuits began—lawsuits that totaled more than 200 million dollars (in 1980 dollars), enough to bankrupt any but those with the deepest of deep pockets. As a result of the tragic MGM Grand fire that might have been prevented had the entire building been fitted with sprinklers, the state of Nevada has enacted some of the strictest fire prevention building code laws in the United States.

Money may talk elsewhere; in Las Vegas it screams. Property on The Strip is far too valuable to remain dormant for very long. The burned-out MGM Grand Hotel was sold.

And the bulldozers rolled in. Under new ownership and stricter building codes, the building was repaired and rebuilt. When the transformation was complete, the hotel/casino became known as Bally's Las Vegas.

From the first came reports of unexplained weeping and screaming in certain areas of the upper-floor hallways. Could this be the ghostly cries of those who perished in the MGM fire decades ago? Some ghost investigators believe it is. And what of the disoriented apparitions that have been reported in certain areas? While some might argue that these sights and sounds are nothing more than imagination, others who have experienced them aren't so sure.

"I don't care what anyone says. I know what I saw," one person explained. "It was misty bluish green, about the height of a tall woman. One minute she was there. And the next she was gone. There is no other explanation for me. That was a ghost."

It is only fair to mention that a new MGM Grand Las Vegas was eventually built; it stands a few blocks from where the original once stood.

Las Vegas Hilton

Legalized gambling was still very much a Nevada-only activity when the International Hotel opened in July 1969. It was the largest hotel in the world, and no expense had been spared. With a price tag of more than $60 million, the palatial International boasted white marble throughout its twenty-four floors and a 30,000 square-foot casino. But savvy gaming execs realized it would take more than that to draw the money and the crowds. So they resorted to the tried-and-true Vegas hook; they booked a top-name entertainer, velvety voiced Barbra Streisand, to wow the opening-night crowd. And that she did. Star power, in Vegas it works every time. During her engagement, the glamorous Ms. Streisand performed before a packed house that included the governor of Nevada, two senators, TV comedian Lucille Ball, and other notables of the day.

When Streisand's stint ended, Elvis Presley sauntered in. Thirteen years had passed since his last performance in Las Vegas. Gone was the swivel-hipped youngster who shocked television viewers with his antics on the old Ed Sullivan Show one Sunday night in 1956. His naiveté long vanished, Elvis was on top of his game. He had met the challenge of being an aging teen idol by discovering a new persona within himself. Skintight leather pants, sequined white polyester jumpsuits, white patent leather boots, and red silk scarves, he wore them all with aplomb.

Elvis broke Las Vegas attendance records that summer at the International; every one of his fifty-eight consecutive shows was a sellout. While he performed for standing-room-only crowds in the two-thousand-seat showroom, he resided in the penthouse on the thirtieth floor. Today the penthouse is still known as the Elvis Suite.

During the early 1970s the International Hotel was sold to Hilton Hotels and renamed the Las Vegas Hilton. Elvis continued pulling in the crowds until his last performance in December 1976. He was the King, and still a major draw.

But the Grim Reaper takes us all, without regard for talent, wealth, and fame. We will never know whether or not Elvis would have endured, as other ageless performers like Tony Bennett, or retired to live out his life in peaceful anonymity. On August 16, 1977, he died in the bathroom of his Memphis home. He was forty-two years old. In honor of the King's contribution to the Hilton, the hotel erected a bronze statue of him a year later. On hand for the unveiling and dedication ceremonies were his father Vernon and ex-wife Priscilla. The statue is in the Hilton lobby.

The first reported sightings of Elvis at the Hilton happened shortly after his death. In his autobiography *Once Before I Go,* longtime Las Vegas entertainer Wayne Newton tells of seeing the deceased Presley in the audience during one of his performances. He is not the only person to have had the pleasure of seeing the ghostly King. Sightings most often occur in the backstage area where, according to one former employee, he and the phantom Elvis crossed paths one morning years ago.

"I have seen hundreds of Elvis impersonators, some good, some not so good. When I saw him I thought, 'Man, if this guy's not a dead ringer for Elvis, I don't know who is. He's got the same way of walking and is easily one of the best Elvis impersonators I've ever seen.' I was fixing to tell him so when he walked up to me. We got within a foot of one another, and all of a sudden I felt so cold, like the heat had gone off or something. I started to ask if he noticed it too, when he just dissolved right there in front of me. I know it sounds crazy, but that's the best way I can describe it."

In fairness to all those ghost hunters seeking Elvis, it should be mentioned that the King's apparition has also been reported at his Graceland home as well as other locations. However, here in Las Vegas he is as popular as he ever was. Any Elvis impersonator worth his sequins will tell you this city still admires Elvis. And it could be this very admiration that keeps the ghostly Elvis ever near. Then too, it could be a strong desire to remain where the action is or the memories of *Viva Las Vegas* when he and his beautiful costar Ann-Margaret took the city by storm.

According to some, Elvis may not be the only ghost at the Hilton. Early in the evening of February 11, 1981, a disgruntled employee deliberately started a fire in an eighth-floor lounge area. As flames leaped up the sides of the building, firefighters averted tragedy by using techniques they had learned in the disastrous MGM Grand fire. When the blaze was contained, eight people were dead, and several others were injured.

A few years ago a woman reported watching a handsome young couple as they sashayed through the casino. She smiled, remembering her own long-ago honeymoon days. *How sweet,* she thought, *a couple of starry-eyed newlyweds.*

The smile was wiped from her face when the couple stopped, passionately kissed, and then calmly walked into thin air.

Luxor

Themed hotels have been a mainstay of Las Vegas since the 1940s when Cowboy Western was hot stuff. The long gone Rancho Las Vegas and Last Frontier accommodated with establishments that bespoke boots and saddles and wagon wheels and knotty pine times at the old log cabin. Then Benjamin "Bugsy" Siegel came along and forced hotel casinos into a new direction of sophistication. Still it was the theme that held the power to entice, and so it has endured.

When King Tut's Tomb in Egypt was opened and plundered in 1922 it's a safe bet that no one was thinking of future gambling establishments in faraway Nevada. It doesn't matter; the boy king would no doubt be proud to know that the Luxor features a full-scale reproduction of his tomb. In keeping with the ancient Egyptian theme, the interior of the pyramid-shaped Luxor boasts the largest atrium in the world and is decorated with reproductions of artifacts from Luxor and Karnak Temple.

But it is the Luxor's exterior that causes the most comments. According to some, the sphinx that faces east toward the rising sun should actually be facing westward. This innocent disregard for ancient tradition has cursed the city and brought bad luck, they say. And if that's not enough, some insist that the world's most powerful beam of light located on the top of the pyramid should be capped for the very same reason. Never mind that the light shines so many miles up into the night sky that astronauts were able to pick out Las Vegas, or that pilots hundreds of miles away can also see it.

Given all the Luxor's ancient Egyptian décor, one might think its ghosts would be from that time period. But this doesn't seem to be the case. According to a long-held Las Vegas rumor, the Luxor was built atop a mob dumping ground; those who "cracked wise" to the wrong person were quickly dispatched to the next world and their bodies unceremoniously buried here.

The ghost most often associated with the Luxor is that of a worker who was accidentally killed during construction of the $375 million hotel/casino in 1993. Keeping him company is the specter of a young woman who committed suicide there shortly after the hotel/casino opened.

In leaping to her death, she used the Luxor's unique design to her advantage. The 120,000-square-foot ground-floor casino area is surrounded by its 4,407 hotel rooms. Instead of looking outward, the room windows face the casino area. Like Denver's famous Brown Hotel, the Luxor is designed so that people can walk out into the hallways on each floor level and look down at the main floor. This permits an unusual view of the casino action below.

To get to and from their rooms, guests take elevators, or inclinators, as they are so dubbed at the Luxor, that travel at a thirty-nine-degree angle. On the day of her death, the woman took the inclinator to one of the upper floors and gazed down at the casino a moment. Then, without warning, she jumped. She landed near the all-you-can-eat buffet, which was quickly closed. Employees in that area were cautioned to remain tight lipped and were sent home for the day. Time is money; the investigation was quickly completed, and employees were urged to be discreet. The area was thoroughly cleaned and sanitized. And the buffet was relocated to another part of the casino where it continues serving up pasta, salad, and other budget-friendly buffet staples.

And yet, on numerous occasions a ghostly woman has been spotted in the area where the buffet once stood. Those who have seen her describe a young woman in a bright red garment. By all accounts, she appears to be very sad. She's not the only jumper. A few years ago a young man dove off one of the top-floor landings and crashed to ground at the reservations desk. His ghost is also said to roam the casino.

Suicides and deaths by natural causes have probably

A glimpse of downtown before the high-rises

occurred at every hotel and motel in the world. Throw in those unfortunate gangsters whose bones may molder deep beneath this sparkling black glass pyramid, and you've got the possibility for a lot of paranormal activity.

Could the ghostly middle-aged man in the striped brown suit be the victim of a long ago mob hit? His apparition has been seen several times aimlessly wandering the hallways of the upper floors. If you don't get out of his way, some claim, he will walk right through you; and when he does, it is like an ice block. Others who've encountered him say he vanishes rather than step aside. All agree that he seems a bit preoccupied and angry. Years ago a local paranormal aficionado sought to investigate this ghostly gent further. The request was nixed even before the last words tumbled from the requester's mouth.

The Mirage

Think opulent Polynesian décor: waterfalls, grottos, a

lagoon, and tropical gardens. There is no question why a ghost might decide to stop by and set up housekeeping at this resort. But why haunt one of the women's bathrooms? With more than three thousand rooms at its disposal, it seems odd that the ghost on premises has chosen to camp out at that particular location. But some insist that is exactly the case.

It all started a few years ago when the automatic faucet sensors started to turn themselves on and off. One night a startled housekeeping employee was so shaken by the bizarre turn of events, she blamed a ghostly presence and refused to ever again work alone in that bathroom. Could it be the workings of a prank-playing ghost? After all, it's not unheard of for a ghost to hang out in a bathroom. Then again, it's also not unheard of for automatic faucet sensors to malfunction. Without any sightings, or other phenomena, the jury is still out on the bathroom ghost. And until someone steps up to the sink and admits to having seen the annoying specter, I'm betting that any spirit in residence here is down at the lagoon, enjoying the tropics, Vegas style.

The Tropicana

Las Vegas is a fast-paced city; if you're doing something in a New York second, you're moving too slow here. This accounts for the locals' propensity to refer to this resort hotel as the Trop. Likewise the street named after the hotel is also called Trop. The hotel is one of the few vestiges from back in the day when the Rat Pack was cool and the mob had its fingers in the tills.

Times change; the Sands, the Dunes, and the Desert Inn are gone. Remodeled, enlarged, and renovated, the Trop remains. And so does its mainstay, the Folies Bergere, the oldest show of its kind in Las Vegas. Considered very naughty when first produced at the Trop nearly fifty years ago, the

Folies was dubbed "The Show that made Paris Famous."

It was wildly successful. How could a show that featured shapely showgirls in scanty sequined costumes, feathers, and little else be otherwise? Being the hot place, stars came and went. "Dahling"-dropping, diamond-drenched Zsa Zsa Gabor was here, as was the buxom, media-hungry Jayne Mansfield, Hollywood leading lady Joan Crawford, and pop singer Eddie Fisher, who crooned to his current lady love, Elizabeth Taylor.

Those in the know say the paranormal phenomenon seems to be centered on an occasional purple haze that is said to sometimes appear in front of the Trop. Photos taken in that area often bear a large purple anomaly. Light refraction, mishandling of film, or any number of factors may be to blame for the mysterious purple haze. Or, as has been suggested, the purple haze could be the apparition of a former Folies Bergere showgirl still craving the limelight and an audience's admiration.

The Stratosphere

The Stratosphere Tower (the Strat in locals' lingo) is 1,149 feet tall, making it the tallest observation tower in the United States. Conceived by Las Vegas casino owner and businessman Bob Stupak, the Stratosphere is an example of what can be achieved with big dreams and bigger bucks.

There's no doubt about it, the views are breathtaking from the revolving restaurant, gift shops, and observation windows, especially after the sun goes down. The roller coaster rides on top the tower are only for the bravest of souls. It is a long way down . . . And yet, several people have chosen to leap to their deaths from this structure since it was opened in 1995. One of them was a young man who is said to haunt the ground-level casino.

"When I first saw him I didn't realize that I was looking

at a ghost," said a former employee, "but afterwards, I remembered that he was a bit pale and sickly. He was always over by the elevator about the same time every shift . . . It was close to Halloween, and we were all talking about ghosts and that sort of thing. Then one of the cocktail waitresses said she had seen the ghost of a man who jumped from the tower, so I asked her what he looked like. The man she described was exactly what I had been seeing."

Stories of ghostly goings-on in this area have been told since well before the Stratosphere was ever erected. Some say that two Native Americans were killed so violently on this spot long ago that they haunt the location to this very day. A few of those who work in the outdoor area of the property have told of hearing soft whisperings and mutterings that seem to emanate from thin air. One woman claimed to have seen a man appear from out of nowhere and stare sternly at her. Terrified, she ran screaming from him, but when she looked back there was no one there. Taking no chances, she has made it a point never to be alone in that area of the grounds again. When asked if she had encountered a ghost, she said, "Well of course I did! People don't all of a sudden appear like that."

Well . . . not unless they happen to be magician's assistants.

Golden Nugget

An aura of old Las Vegas still remains at the Golden Nugget in the Fremont Experience. Opened in the summer of 1946 in the downtown area of Las Vegas known as Glitter Gulch, the Golden Nugget was considered the most luxurious casino in town. But are there any ghosts in residence? According to a former employee a shadowy figure followed her around the casino floor during her graveyard shift years ago.

"The thing is, I only saw her just that once . . . I'm pretty

The Golden Nugget circa 1947

sure it was a woman. She was in some kind of distress . . . The weird thing is no one seemed to notice her but me. I asked one of the bartenders if he saw her; he looked at me like I was crazy. So I didn't ask anyone else."

During a segment of the television series *Dead Famous,* sensitive Chris Fleming stayed in the Frank Sinatra Suite and claimed to have made contact with Old Blue Eyes while there. Less famous, but no less ghostly, is the dark wispy figure some have reportedly seen in the casino late at night. This could be a ghost who has wandered over from the tragic explosion at the Orbit Inn.

The Sahara

When the Sahara was built, a steak would set you back a buck, and Vegas Vic, in all his neon glory, welcomed visitors to downtown's Glitter Gulch. The 240-room hotel/casino's theme was desert and stars, big-name stars that could pull in the money and the crowds. Martha Raye, Bobby Darin, Mae West, and Connie Francis were but a few who headlined in the Casbar Theater Lounge. The Congo Room would come later. The Sahara attracted the stars; among them was Elvis, who supposedly spent some time there with redheaded burlesque star Tempest Storm back in the day.

When its twenty-four-story tower was built in the early 1960s it was proclaimed the tallest hotel building in ten Western states. Unfortunately, this boast attracted at least one person intent on suicide.

The sun was just coming up over Sunrise Mountain when he finally decided to end it all. He took a cab to the Sahara and went up to the twenty-third floor. Security guards chased him off three times; each time he returned. Finally he eased out onto the ledge and gazed out across the valley. And then he jumped.

Some who've stayed on this floor have experienced cold drafts and the feeling that someone is creeping up behind them. "It was almost as if someone was trying to whisper in my ear," one person explained.

Moulin Rouge Memories

Back in the day, people of color often referred to Las Vegas as the Mississippi of the West. They had good reason to do so. Until the Moulin Rouge was opened in 1955, African Americans were not always welcome in the large Las Vegas hotel/casinos. Oh sure they could wait tables, cook meals, and change the sheets, but sitting down at the blackjack table was another matter entirely. This terrible injustice didn't apply only to the guests and the hired help; African American celebrities like Pearl Bailey and Nat King Cole also found themselves facing the same discrimination. The message, while not spoken, was clear: Entertain our paying customers all you want, but when the set is over, go on back to the other side of town.

Many celebrities still remember the days of being forced to find room and board on the Westside, which was predominately African American, while performing at one of the big hotels on The Strip. The opening of the Moulin Rouge in May 1955 would help to change all that.

Opening night at the Moulin Rouge brought integration

to Las Vegas for the first time. The club was packed with people of color as well as whites. Coming together was good and right. The June 20, 1955, issue of *Life* magazine would feature African American showgirls on its cover, and a story of the Moulin Rouge. Change was in the wind that swept across the Vegas Valley.

While the Moulin Rouge was rocking, someone discovered the body of a young saxophonist in a field less than a mile from the famed nightclub. His neck had been broken, the result of a fall during a wild party of alcohol and drugs. But the show must go on. A suitable replacement was found, and the saxophone player was all but forgotten.

It mattered little that the young man had worked so hard to get here. Life is for the living. So celebrities and notables of the day came and went. And the opening celebrations went forward.

The Moulin Rouge has been gone many years. Yet some have heard the sounds of laughter, and of music, and a saxophone solo that could knock your socks off, coming from the deserted building late at night. Perhaps it is a spectral saxophonist determined to grab just one more moment in the spotlight.

Financially, the Moulin Rouge was a disaster. The nightclub closed six months after its much-anticipated opening. Various people took over its ownership, one of whom was Sarann Knight-Preddy, the first black woman to hold a Nevada gaming license. Five years after its historic opening, the Moulin Rouge was closed. But the nightclub again made history when it was chosen as the site of a meeting between civil rights leaders and casino owners. As a result of that March 26, 1960, meeting, African Americans were, for the first time, allowed to gamble at Strip and downtown hotel/casinos.

The Moulin Rouge was operated solely as a motel for many years. There may have been a ghost in at least one of its units. A woman named Myra told the following story about a stay at the Moulin Rouge.

In 1975 we were living in Los Angeles, and my folks were living in Las Vegas. As a surprise birthday present my husband took me to Vegas for a visit. We were on a very tight budget, so we got a room at the Moulin Rouge. It was old and rundown, but it was about all we could afford at the time. We planned to spend a night of gambling by ourselves, then call my parents the next day.

We were just getting ready to call it a night when I won tickets to a floor show at the Tropicana. It was a good show, but it lasted longer than we thought. We were half asleep by the time we got back to the room. I am a sound sleeper, but the sound of someone saying "please no . . . please don't" woke me up. My husband was snoring away, and I sat up and looked across at the other bed. For a moment I was disoriented. Then I remembered that we were given a room with two double beds. All of a sudden a woman appeared on the other bed. I could see right through her so I had a pretty good idea that I was either dreaming or she was some kind of ghost or something. She was crying softly and saying over and over, "please no, please don't."

I looked at the clock. It was a quarter to four. Too late to call my parents and too early to get up.

"Just go away," I said, and turned from the bed. I must have been tired; I fell right back to sleep.

The next morning I called my mom, and she was horrified when she found out we were staying at the Moulin Rouge. "You two had better come here and stay with us tonight."

"That Moulin Rouge is a rough place. There's lots of dope and killings; why just last week a girl was murdered there in one of the rooms," she said.

My heart started pounding. "Were there any pictures of her in the paper?"

"I don't think so. Why?"

"Just curious," I lied. There was no point in telling my mother what I had seen.

In 1992 the Moulin Rouge was listed in the National Register of Historic Places. A devastating fire destroyed most of the building in 2003. Only the sign Moulin Rouge remains; that, and its ghosts.

The Dunes' Spectral Keno Runner

The Keno game is like the lottery. There are eighty numbers to choose from, but only twenty are drawn. In recent years, the game has lost its popularity to the fast-paced card games in the pit and to the slot machines. Back in the day, Keno brought customers to the casinos. There were always job openings for Keno runners.

No one wanted to make a career of running Keno. It was too grueling for the money that was paid. An entry-level position, the job of Keno runner was eight hours of running throughout the casino, picking up customer tickets, taking them to the Keno counter for registering, and returning them to the right customer. This was not so easy when a runner had picked up tickets from thirty or so customers. It's no wonder that Keno runners were always looking for another job, any job.

In the fall of 1975 she was at last twenty-one years old. One of the first things she did as a legal adult, besides play the slots, was give her notice at the fast-food restaurant where she worked. Then she applied for a job as a Keno runner at the Dunes. A few days later she was on the floor and in training. Stamina, patience, a good personality, and an excellent memory, she had them all, and soon she was on her way to being a top Keno runner.

No one in Keno figured her long for the game. She was just too pretty not to catch the eyes of the pit boss and the bar manager. One or the other was sure to ask that she be transferred to his department. Besides her good looks, the young woman was bubbly, enthusiastic, and kind; everybody who knew her liked her. She would be missed when that transfer finally came.

It never did. One night after work, she stopped at the convenience store near her home and walked in on a robbery. Startled, the robber shot and killed the store clerk, then turned the gun on her. The Keno department was stunned. Death shouldn't happen to someone so young

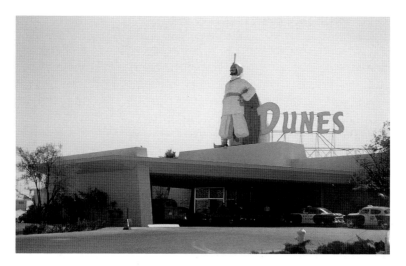

The Dunes during the 1960s

and vibrant and so full of life. But life isn't always fair. The young woman they all liked was gone.

But was she? The first person to see her was another Keno runner who swore she had seen her in the ladies' bathroom. And then a writer on the graveyard shift saw her at the Keno counter; someone else saw her in the restaurant and in the pit. Years passed, the city grew, and the old had to make way for the new. Eventually the Dunes was demolished; hopefully the young Keno runner has moved on.

Chapter 2

Public Places and Phantom Faces

Schools

Three cheers for the old Alma Mater: rah, rah, rah. With its ivy-covered walls and musty smelling libraries, it was all good. Even with the endless homework, the exams, and term papers, most of us fondly remember our school days. Even if you don't, many people do. This might be why so many schools are haunted.

Las Vegas Academy

Work on the Boulder Dam (later renamed Hoover Dam) began in earnest in 1930. Aside from preventing flooding in Southern Arizona, Nevada, and California, the creation of the dam provided jobs for thousands of men who had seen employment vanish in the wake of the Great Depression. Rather than live in nearby Boulder City, with its stringent rules and regulations, some workers chose to settle with their families in Las Vegas, thirty miles from the job site.

As word got around, more people moved in, the city's population surged to more than five thousand, and the need for more schools increased. Las Vegas High School, built on land deeded to the city by the Union Pacific Railroad, was the city's first high school. It's hard to imagine now, but some worried that the new school, located at 315 S. Seventh Street, was too far out of town. They needn't have. The beautiful Art Deco-design high school would continue to graduate students for the next sixty years.

In 1994 the school was converted to the Las Vegas Academy of International Studies. The nationally recognized academy offers its more than fourteen hundred students a program of international studies, visual arts, and performing arts. According to a long-held rumor, there is also a ghost in residence at the Performing Arts Center, or the PAC, as students and locals refer to it.

The Performing Arts Center was built as Las Vegas High School's auditorium in the early 1950s and is one of the oldest such structures in the city. With 1,427 seats, the PAC is a popular rental theater with locals.

Years before Las Vegas High School graduated its last class there was talk of a ghostly old gent who haunted the school's auditorium. Someone started calling the ghost Mr. Petrie, and the name stuck. There are numerous theories as to who Mr. Petrie was in life. He is believed to be the ghost of an elderly man who perished in a horrible house fire nearby; others claim he is a long-ago student, or a

Front door of the Las Vegas Academy

former teacher who merely wants to make certain that everything is as it should be.

It all depends on which version of the story you choose to believe—or what experience you have with him. "He was a teacher," one woman insists. "My friends and I saw him, big as you please, in the auditorium several years ago. There were only three of us in the place. We were talking loudly about some boy, and then we started to laugh. About then we saw this old man in suit and tie coming right toward us. I never will forget how intensely cold it got all of sudden. We started shivering, it was so cold. He glared at us and held his finger to his lips in a sign to be quiet. Thinking he was a teacher, we naturally complied. He got up to where we were sitting, and that's when we noticed that he didn't have any feet. He was floating a few inches off the floor. We ran out of there so fast. Oh yes, he was a teacher. He had that air about him."

Apparently the ghostly educator is not very camera shy. He well may be the only ghost to grace the pages of a high school yearbook. According to some, the 1968 yearbook of Las Vegas High School contains a photograph of Mr. Petrie himself.

Historians point out that a family with a name similar to Petrie did reside in the area where the academy now stands. Whether or not the paterfamilias died in a house fire is not known.

Meanwhile, the hijinks keep happening. As if opening night jitters are not bad enough, the mischievous Mr. Petrie occasionally lets loose with a string of ill-timed pranks. He has been accused of causing lights to flicker and icy breezes to waft through the auditorium. Likewise noisily slamming doors during a performance and misplacing items are also his doing. While some insist there is nothing more going on here than vivid imaginations working overtime, others claim there is definitely a presence lurking in the Performing Arts Center.

But not so fast with your ghost hunting gear; the academy is not anxious to have ghost investigators snooping out spirits.

Treem Elementary

"Success for Kids" is the motto of Harriet Treem Elementary School in Henderson. Approximately six hundred students in grades three through five attend the sixteen-year-old school that was nominated for Redbook's America's Best Schools Award.

Tales of a ghostly little girl lurking here in this atmosphere of learning and exploring have been going around for many years. No one knows who she is, or why she chose to haunt the school. Witnesses say she usually cries for help when she realizes that someone has seen her. Most reports say her attire is of a long-ago pioneer time, but it is her glowing phantom-like face that is always most distinguishable.

She could be nothing more than youthful imagination. But then again, it's not so uncommon for a ghost to take up residence at school. The child might have been a member of an immigrant family that passed through this area over a century ago. She may have died along the way, leaving her heartbroken family no other option but to bury her here beneath the desert sand. And although time has moved on for the rest of the world, the little girl may not realize that she is dead. That is one theory. But there is another more sinister one. The ghostly youngster could well be the victim of a long-ago unsolved murder, crying out for justice. Maybe one day the mystery of the white-faced ghost girl of Treem Elementary will be solved.

Vo-Tech High School

Vo-Tech, located in southeast Las Vegas, is one of three career and technical high schools in the Clark County school district that offer students the opportunity to earn certificates in culinary arts, computer graphics, construction, and nursing. It is not for everybody; students must maintain a C average to stay enrolled, and homework is required. There may not be a football team at Vo-Tech, but according to rumor, there is a ghost.

Just why the ghostly old man, seen standing by one of the outside doors, appears only after dark is anybody's guess. Perhaps nighttime is when he died, quit work, or took his lunch break.

One person who witnessed the old man's ghost told the following story: "I got turned around and stopped the car to check my map. When I saw this old guy standing by the door I thought he was a janitor. He was wearing this brown jumpsuit thing with a name embroidered in yellow on the front of it, but I couldn't make it out. Thinking he was a janitor or something, I asked him what time it was, and he just sorta smirked at me and walked right through the door. He looked as solid as you or I. But when he went through that door . . . I tell you that's something I'm not apt to forget. It really gave me the chills."

Museums

It's easy to see why a museum might be haunted by ghosts; especially if, as some paranormal researchers believe, people can become so attached to their worldly possessions that even death cannot separate them. Educational as they may be, what are museums but the repositories of historic remnants and the possessions of long-dead people?

Clark County Museum

At $1.50 admission, the Clark County Museum is one of the best bargains in Las Vegas. Offering the original depot from Boulder City, circa 1932, a real caboose, a boxcar, a baggage car, historic mining implements, and exhibits of early Las Vegas, the museum is a great place to spend a day. Ghost hunters have only to walk onto shady Heritage Street where the main exhibits are historic houses, complete with household furnishings, classic cars, and a travel trailer in some of the driveways.

These five houses and a print shop were rescued from demolition in various locations throughout Las Vegas and brought here to the museum grounds where they were restored and refurnished to fit their specific time in the city's history.

This was history that Las Vegans cared about preserving. With demolition imminent, the Beckley House became the first house on Heritage Street. Said to be one of the most haunted, the California-style bungalow was built downtown at 120 S. Fourth Street for Will Beckley, who paid $2,500 for it in 1912.

Witnesses have reported seeing an elderly man and a ghostly little girl who stand near the staircase that leads to the attic. According to museum staff, there may be a prank-playing spirit in residence as well. Unseen hands sometimes muss the carefully made bed. One minute the bedspread is nice and neat; the next it is rumpled. And what about the mysterious butt print? No matter how often employees straightened the antique quilt bedspread, an unexplained butt print would appear.

"It looked like someone had just sat down on it," one employee said.

Museum employees are at a loss to explain the strange moans that have emanated from the empty house. The first time the sounds were heard, maintenance employees were called to find the problem and fix it. They worked half the afternoon, checking the air conditioner thoroughly; it was not the source of the noise, nor could they find any other explanation.

The Giles/Barcus House was originally built in Goldfield during its boom in 1905. Edwin Schofield Giles and his wife Edith Corliss Giles purchased the house in 1928. Their daughter Edith Giles Barcus brought the house to Las Vegas in 1955, where it served as an antique shop on the corner of Hacienda and Giles Streets for many years. Many who visit the house say there is something very eerie about it.

A visitor said, "I walked in and distinctly heard the

sounds of someone playing a piano. I thought maybe it was coming from the sound system, but when I said something about the particular song, my husband shook his head. He hadn't heard any music in there."

Another visitor saw an elderly woman sitting in the corner of the house:

> It was the middle of summer. It had to be a hundred and ten in the shade. There was this old woman wearing a heavy dark velvet dress. She was bent over some type of needlework. I thought she was a docent so I waved and said, "Hi there, you must be sweltering in that costume."
>
> She didn't even look up. So I thought she was taking a break, and left her to it. Later I was talking to the woman in the gift shop and told her about the old docent. When she told me there was no one like that working in the Giles/Barcus house, I knew that I had seen a ghost.

The Goumand House was originally built in 1931 on S. Seventh Street and was bought by Las Vegas businessman Prosper J. Goumand who, along with several partners, owned the Boulder Club, a casino on Fremont Street. Goumand, his wife, and granddaughter lived in the home that was considered luxurious in its time with a full basement and one of the city's first private swimming pools.

Some psychics who have visited the house claim there is sadness about it. "Nothing mean or negative," said one woman, "but there is definitely an overwhelming sadness here."

A slender young woman has been seen standing in the doorway of the Goumand House several times. The moment someone speaks to her, the woman vanishes into thin air. Some people see a large ghostly black cat scampering down the hallway of the house. Thinking he was a stray who had somehow wandered in, a visitor stooped and tried to pick up the cat, only to come up with an armful of air.

As they do in many haunted houses, doors open and shut of their own volition. But most of the strange activity seems to center around the sewing room where ceiling lights have snapped and broken in their sockets. On a cold and windy afternoon two museum employees were working in the sewing room. After they had carefully laid out the items that needed to be sewn and ironed, one of the women plugged in the iron and commented about the room being so cold.

"Maybe they should take a look at the heating system," the other woman said absently. At that moment the iron was angrily flung from the ironing board. Neither woman said a word. It wasn't the first time they had experienced something out of the ordinary here.

The Townsite House was built in 1942 as temporary shelter for workers at the magnesium processing plant. A lovely pomegranate tree grows in its front yard. Don't let that fool you. Some sensitives claim the Townsite House is the house with the most energy; not all of it is positive.

A visiting sensitive shuddered the moment she walked through the front door. Overcome with sadness, she felt that paranormal activity might be connected in some way to the child's room; it was here that she picked up what she called "a strong almost negative feeling." She turned and headed for the door. "This house holds some dark secrets," she explained.

With all this reportedly paranormal action going on at the museum, it is only natural that ghost investigative teams would want to visit. When Las Vegas Paranormal Investigations conducted a three-hour ghost investigation of the houses on Heritage Street, interesting things started to happen almost as soon as the team arrived.

Brand new batteries went dead inside the houses, only to revive and work once outside (a common occurrence in haunted locations), a camera snapped photos on its own accord, and temperature fluctuations were significant. While there were no actual sightings of ghostly residents, the group concluded there is something paranormal going on here on Heritage Street.

The Atomic Testing Museum

He may have been assigned to the Nevada Proving Grounds. Perhaps he found his way here because an item on display at the museum once belonged to him. Those who have caught a glimpse of him say that his face is horribly scarred and is almost covered by the sort of dark goggles that military personnel were issued for viewing atomic tests. Attired in decades-old army gear, he is the ghost of the Atomic Testing Museum. And he keeps his lonely vigil, belonging to another time and place.

Through its displays, artifacts, and first-person narratives, the Atomic Testing Museum tells the story of the Nevada Test Site. It is a story not without irony.

After looking at several other locations for testing nuclear weapons, the Atomic Energy Commission finally settled on a 680-square-mile area in the Southern Nevada desert known as Yucca Flats. President Harry S. Truman approved the establishment of the Nevada Proving Grounds on January 11, 1951, and testing was a go.

In May 1953, with Operation Upshot Knothole, atomic testing began in earnest at the Nevada Proving Grounds. Sixty-five miles away, Las Vegans felt the rumbling explosions and saw the mushroom clouds as they rose in the sky. The nuclear age had arrived. And everyone was excited. Seeing the opportunity to turn a quick buck, Sin City businessmen called in their PR teams and capitalized on the events. Aside from offering customers a pair of shades to watch the not-so-faraway mushroom clouds whirling up into the atmosphere, they christened new atomic cocktails, the atomic bomb boogie, and atomic hairstyles. Was there ever a better tourist attraction?

This was during the 1950s and the Cold War. Then it occurred to Americans that if we were testing such deadly devices, so were our enemies. And no one wanted to meet death via some enemy's atomic bomb. A bomb shelter was the answer, and suddenly a well-stocked shelter became the new status symbol. Meanwhile promoters were lapping it up in Las Vegas as testing continued at the Nevada Proving Grounds. No one gave a thought to the effects of downwind fallout, as they designed postcards and crowned a new Miss Atomic Bomb. In all, more than nine hundred nuclear tests would be conducted during the next forty years. One hundred of those would be above-ground tests.

If you want to see it all up close and personal, regular monthly tours of the Nevada Test Site are now being offered. You won't be allowed to drive there yourself; no way. Hop on the bus that leaves the Atomic Testing Museum at seven in the morning and returns around four in the afternoon. But this isn't any spur-of-the-moment tour. For security reasons, you have to apply for the tour well in advance of your intended visit. If you forget, you're out of luck; you won't be riding on the bus.

Read and obey the list of no-nos: no cameras, no recorders, no laptops, no cell phones, and no firearms. What did you expect? You can't have it all. Once you are past the security screening, you will find the tour enjoyable and informative.

Parks

A park may seem like a strange place for a haunting, but then, a haunting could be considered strange in and of itself, by some. Who knows what events occurred a century or more ago on the parcels of land now designated as parks?

Floyd Lamb Park at Tule Springs

In 1941 casino owner Prosper Goumand bought this land and began developing it as a dude ranch for divorcees who needed a place to while away their required six-weeks residencies in the lap of luxury, Western style. The Las Vegas divorce industry had been on the upswing ever since Rhea Langham came to town in 1939 seeking to sever matrimonial ties with movie idol Clark Gable.

With a warmer clime and easier access to Los Angeles, Las Vegas stood to snatch the title of Divorce Capital of the World from Reno. This is where astute businessmen like Goumand stepped in. His Tule Springs Ranch offered divorcees with plenty of disposable income a swimming pool, hayrides, shooting ranges, nightly entertainment, and just possibly a chance at romance. When the divorce industry fizzled, and the dudes stopped coming, the ranch was put to use as a cattle ranch. In 1974 Tule Springs Ranch became the Floyd Lamb State Park. Once a safe refuge miles from the city, thanks to the area's continued sprawl today the former ranch is about twenty minutes from The Strip. Long before those eager for a quick fix for a faulty marriage came to this area, people resided in the region. Fossils indicate that ancient humans lived and hunted in the area 10,000 years ago. In fact, the park is said to be one of best Pleistocene paleontology sites in Western North America. That's a lot of history, and perhaps an explanation for the group of shadowy figures reportedly seen here after dark. Granted this is a delightful area to explore, but would-be ghost hunters are warned, the park is strictly a day-use-only park. Come picnic and explore all you want. But any ghost hunting will have to be done during daylight hours. Do you honestly believe that ghosts only come out once the sun goes down? A visit here might change your mind.

Green Valley Park

As parks go, Green Valley Park in Henderson is small. This doesn't mean there couldn't be a ghost or two lurking here. Now please, whatever you do, don't try to tell passengers aboard Robert Allen's Haunted Vegas bus tour that the Green Valley Park is not haunted. Too many unexplained ghostly photos and EVP have been captured here for anyone to believe that. But just who is the ghost that shows up in these photos?

According to one old story, a pioneer girl was murdered where the picnic tables now stand. And yes, some of the EVP does sound like a young girl calling for help. But there are also those who say that the ghost of Green Valley Park is an elderly woman who, like the pioneer girl, was murdered in the vicinity.

Dowsers on the Haunted Vegas tour are often drawn to an area closer to the middle of the park. "Underground water," said one dowser from the East Coast.

"No way, dude! There's no underground water within a couple hundred miles," a native Las Vegan informed him.

"Well, maybe it is another ghost," the East Coast dowser suggested.

So how many ghosts does it take to haunt a park? Long-dead pioneer girl, or old woman? Take your pick. It could be that one, or both of them, is haunting the Green Valley Park.

Streets

All across the country urban street legends abound, legends like vanishing automobiles and headless motorcyclists. The most prevalent is the old story of the damsel in distress. This hitchhiker is always beautiful. She has to be beautiful; otherwise, why would anyone stop and give her a ride? The hitchhiker usually appears in the pouring rain, and only lives down the road. Invariably she leaves an article of clothing behind in the car (usually a coat or sweater). When the Good Samaritan attempts to find her and return her lost gear, he discovers that she has been dead for years.

Las Vegas has its share of gorgeous showgirls. But there are no hitchhiking ghosts here in Sin City. There is, however, the story of the screaming specter. There is nothing beautiful about this elderly woman ghost who accosts slow-moving automobiles on Sandhill Road in the wee hours of the morning. If you see her, don't stop! Just get out of her neighborhood. That's all she really wants.

The haunted flood tunnels on Sandhill and Charleston are nearby. They are said to be inhabited by the ghosts of a young couple who died in a fiery motorcycle crash years ago. On certain nights, especially the anniversary of their fateful ride, the sounds of plaintive whispering can be heard in the tunnel. Some even claim to hear the sounds of laughter emanating from the haunted tunnel.

Hmmm. It may be possible for ghosts to return to the scene on the anniversary of their passing, but I'd be willing to bet my commemorative twenty-five-dollar Bugsy Siegel chip that these sounds have nothing whatsoever to do with the motorcycle ghosts.

Blue Diamond Road (Route 160)

If you should be driving along the Blue Diamond Road during the wee hours of the morning, and a man frantically tries to flag you down, don't stop. Don't even look back. He is one of several ghosts who roam this fifty-mile length of highway known to locals as the Highway of Death. Even more frightening is the glowing woman who wanders aimlessly down the middle of the road. When drivers swerve to avoid hitting her, she vanishes. On full-moon nights an elderly couple is said to walk along the road. Those who have seen them say the oldsters appear to be lost or in search of something. Go ahead. Stop if you must. But be warned: this ghostly couple will walk right through you and your vehicle. And when they do so, be prepared for an unearthly chill.

Las Vegans have good reason to call Blue Diamond Road (Route 160), which stretches from Las Vegas to Pahrump, the Highway of Death. Known for a high number of fatal automobile accidents, the once rural road has become congested and dangerous as the population has increased here in the Las Vegas Valley. The sixty-five-miles-per-hour speed limit has been lowered and the road widened in certain locations; still there are those who believe the Blue Diamond Road is so cursed that they refuse to drive on it.

Sixty years ago this area near Blue Diamond was desolate and forgotten. It was the ideal out-of-the-way spot for murderers and mobsters to dump the bodies of their victims. Perhaps some of those victims haunt this highway still.

Seventeen people lost their lives on the Blue Diamond Road during a recent six-month period. Of these, Las Vegas resident and retired porn star Anna Malle (Anna Hotop-Stout) is the most famous. Ms. Malle joined the ranks of those who met their death on the Highway of Death on

January 26, 2006. One sunny afternoon, thirty-eight-year-old Malle did not buckle up when she slid into the passenger seat. Halfway down the highway, the car's driver eased up on the gas and attempted to make a U-turn; at that moment a pickup truck came racing down the road from the opposite direction. It was too late to stop. The truck plowed into the car, killing the beautiful Ms. Malle.

Death on a Downtown Street

He knew this street better than anyone; he had driven over it countless times. Traffic was lighter than usual on this night, so he allowed his mind to wonder as he drove past familiar sights. Lost in thought, he paid little attention to the car in front of him, until the crunch of his vehicle rear-ending its bumper jarred him back to the present.

It was nothing more than a minor fender bender, a nuisance that might make him a few minutes late for his date. But he could explain. Almost cheerfully, he jumped out to inspect the damage. An exchange of names and driver's license numbers and he would be on his way. He

Downtown Las Vegas back in the day

spoke to other driver who remained in his vehicle. While he compared his bumper to that of the other car, a third car came careening around the corner. Before he could jump to safety the speeding car smashed into him, tossing his body twenty feet in the air. He was dead before the ambulance arrived . . .

Even in Las Vegas, which some people perceive as an adult Disneyland, life can be transitory.

Cemeteries

Sleeping Celebrities

Stargazing in cemeteries, why not? Especially if you've come to Las Vegas in search of dearly departed celebrities; plenty of stars rest in peace here.

At least one celebrity has reservations in the hereafter. According to Sin City gossip, Wayne Newton, affectionately known as Mr. Las Vegas, has his final resting spot all picked out and waiting. Now that is planning for the future.

Comedian Redd Foxx, a Las Vegas resident for more than forty years, died unexpectedly in Los Angeles in 1991. Look for his grave just inside and to the left of Palm Memorial East's main entrance. Foxx's real name was John Elroy Sanford, but his stage name appears on his headstone. A red fox's face is carved beside the name Redd Foxx. Following his birth and death dates are the words, "You are my [a red heart is carved here] always."

Also in residence at Palm Memorial East is old-time bootlegger and reputed mobster Moe Dalitz who slumbers in the Garden of Eternal Peace section. When Bugsy Siegel's dream was shattered in a hail of bullets, Dalitz picked up the pieces and helped make the city what it is today. In the late 1940s Dalitz came to Las Vegas and opened the Desert Inn with his business partners. He may have been a friend of the late mobster Meyer Lansky, but Dalitz was a generous man who donated to several local charities throughout his life. His good works did not go unnoticed; the American Cancer Research Center and Hospital named him Humanitarian of the Year in 1976.

No city loves its lore more than Sin City. A longtime favorite story involves Dalitz's testimony during the 1950 Senate Special Committee to Investigate Crime in Interstate Commerce headed by Tennessee Senator Estes Kefauver.

When Kefauver asked Dalitz if his Las Vegas investments were financed by the money he had made as a bootlegger, he replied, "Well, I didn't inherit any money, Senator. If you people wouldn't have drunk it, I wouldn't have bootlegged it."

And while we are on the subject of old-time mobsters, let's not forget that one of gangster Mickey Cohen's girlfriends is in residence in Las Vegas. Blonde bombshell actress Liz Renay reposes at Bunkers Eden Vale Cemetery. Renay was a ringer for her confidante and pal Marilyn Monroe. According to her book *My First 2000 Men,* Renay swapped more than secrets with MM; she romped with the likes of Hollywood heartthrob Cary Grant and baseball legend Joe DiMaggio.

Also taking up space at Bunkers Eden Vale Cemetery is local legend and gambling hall operator Benny Binion. Resting nearby is his son Ted. Ted gained his fame posthumously. His suspicious death and the subsequent *Court TV* coverage of the murder trial of his beautiful and much younger girlfriend focused worldwide attention on the name Binion. The moral is: drugs, don't mix 'em. Ted learned this lesson too late, and it was a deadly mistake. Rest in peace, Ted.

There may be hundreds of Elvis wannabes here in Vegas, but the real-deal King is buried clear across the country at Graceland in Memphis. Don't worry. He's not lonesome tonight. His grave is near those of his mama and daddy. Elvis's longtime manager, Colonel Tom Parker, prefers Sin City. The Colonel spends eternity at Palm Desert Memorial. While you are here you might want to mosey on over and pay your respects to cowboy film star Wild Bill Elliott. Wild Bill starred in a string of Westerns back in the forties and fifties. But the public is a fickle lot. When interest in cowboy flicks waned, Elliott saddled up and headed for Las Vegas and retirement. Ironically, Wild Bill, who earned his living for a time promoting a particular cigarette brand, died of lung cancer in 1965. Gotta light?

What would life be without sports? What would eternity be without sports? Two sports greats sleep the eternal sleep in Paradise Memorial Gardens located at 6200 S. Eastern Avenue.

Heavyweight Champion of the World Sonny Liston's headstone inscription is terse: Charles "Sonny" Liston, 1932-1970 "A Man."

Nearby is another baseball great, pitcher Bo Belinsky. Inscribed on his headstone, along with his birth and death dates, are the words "No hitter 5/5/62." Thus the no hitter he pitched against the Baltimore Orioles for the Los Angeles Angels will never be forgotten.

And so it is. Ashes to ashes, dust to dust. Even celebrities must shuffle off this mortal coil. With apologies to Hollywood, more of them are choosing to stay forever in Sin City in the shadow of the neon.

Sports Venues

Ghostly Golfer

If you plan on retiring to Sin City to play a weekly round of golf, get wise quick. It's early to bed and early to rise for Las Vegas golfers. They have to hit the golf courses very early in the morning before the day's heat intensifies. Living here on the edge of the Mojave Desert, they really don't have any choice. An elderly golfer who got to the course just as the sun was rising told this story of a daylight encounter with the ghostly realm at one of the city's older golf courses:

There was still a little nip in the air. It was enough to make you shiver if you weren't wearing long sleeves. That's what I call perfect golfing weather. The sun was barely up when I got set to tee off. I looked across the green and saw this man walking towards me. What the heck was he doing out there? I wondered. He sure as heck wasn't playing golf. I yelled for him to get out of the way. But he just stood there looking from side to side, like he was lost or something.

I made to swing my driver, and still he didn't budge.

"Hey you! Do you mind moving?" I called to him.

Well, he looks at me like he isn't even seeing me. Then it was like he walked right into nothingness, and was gone. If you're asking what type of clothing he was wearing, or anything like that, I couldn't tell you. No, I don't know what he was, but I can tell you he sure gave me a creepy feeling.

FORE!

Chapter 3
That's Show Biz

We are intrigued by celebrities. The clothes they wear (or don't wear), where they go, who they date and marry is of interest to us. Most of us keep up with our favorite celebs better than we do our next-door neighbors. They are stars. Our neighbors aren't. Our fascination with celebrities never wanes, even after the Grim Reaper has claimed them—especially, after the Grim Reaper has grabbed them. For then, you see, they can't deny the dirt the gossip columnists keep throwing at them. Just because celebrities are dead doesn't mean they aren't newsworthy.

Ask any ghost hunter worth his or her sea salt, and they will tell you: specters of the dead and famous are the most intriguing of all.

Tupac Shakur

It was September 7, 1996. Tupac Shakur and thousands of other fight fans were in Vegas for the World Boxing Association heavyweight title bout between Mike Tyson and Bruce Seldon. The much-anticipated fight was over in 103 seconds, lasting only long enough for Tyson to knock his opponent to the mat twice, win the match by a TKO, and reclaim the heavyweight title he had lost to Buster Douglas in 1990.

As disappointed fans poured from the MGM Grand a fight broke out at the hotel's entrance. Later some would say that Tupac was the impetus for the fight; hotel surveillance tape clearly showed him jumping into the fracas. But a private party at Club 662 was waiting on the other side of town. So he stepped out of the melee, dusted himself off, and was whisked away by his friend Suge Knight in a new black BMW. After a quick stop at his hotel room where Tupac changed into casual partying clothes, they were off again, followed by Tupac's entourage.

Suge Knight was behind the wheel. As he skillfully maneuvered the luxury sedan through the maze of Las Vegas traffic, the handsome Tupac Shakur rode shotgun, mesmerized by the sights and sounds of the city. Headed for a good time, the two men probably laughed and joked and made their plans for the evening. The BMW eased up to the corner of Koval and Flamingo Streets, and a white Cadillac pulled up alongside.

Neither man sensed danger. The Cadillac's occupants had their quarry in site and opened fire. Tupac's plans were shattered with the deafening sound of gunfire and of bullets crashing through the tinted glass windows of the BMW. Instinctively, he tried to crawl to the safety of the backseat. Although he usually wore a bulletproof vest, on this night Shakur had made a fateful decision. It was just too hot to wear the vest. Five bullets found their mark, cutting short a promising career and critically injuring the world-famous actor and rapper.

He lingered six days before giving in to the inevitable; it was Friday the thirteenth. Distraught fans camped outside the hospital awaiting news. When it finally came, they stormed the hospital and the coroner's office wanting a glimpse, just a glimpse, of Tupac in death. Nothing doing! Shakur's family ordered that the remains be cremated ASAP.

It is difficult for fans to let go of their fallen idols. Like Elvis Presley before him, Tupac Shakur is rumored to still be alive somewhere and living it up under an assumed name. As evidence, some fans point to the rap star's lyrics and to the fact that he predicted his own death. However, a published autopsy photo would seem to prove that Shakur is no longer of this world. Or is he?

At least one person claims to have seen the ghostly Tupac at the corner where he was fatally wounded.

"I drive down Koval on my way home from work every night. The first time I saw him I thought, 'That couldn't be; my imagination must be playing tricks on me . . .' Then I saw him another time. Now I'm not so sure."

The ghostly Tupac Shakur has also been spotted in a certain tony Las Vegas neighborhood. His haunt is a nouveau California-style mansion, with plenty of stucco and adobe tile; the million-dollar-plus home and its sapphire-colored pool is surrounded by palms, pines, hedges, and a stone fence. Rumor is that after dark the ghostly rapper occasionally appears on the balcony and stares somberly into the distance.

As a former resident put it, "I first heard about Tupac Shakur's ghost one evening while I was walking my dog. A few of us stopped down the street from Mike Tyson's former home about dusk and watched as a big truck came and hauled away all of Tyson's palm trees. A woman started talking about ghosts and said that Tupac Shakur haunts one of the homes further up the road. She didn't say how she knew about the ghost, and I didn't ask."

Liberace

In 1944 a handsome curly-haired kid from Milwaukee introduced himself to Maxine Lewis, the entertainment director for the Last Frontier. He said his stage name was Liberace, he was a pianist, and a darn good one at that. Maxine Lewis liked what she heard and agreed with the young man's assessment of himself. She signed him to a contract with the Last Frontier, guaranteeing him $750 per week.

But as she watched his first performance, Lewis realized that the charismatic young man had something besides talent. He could hold his audience enthralled better than anyone she had ever seen. Yes, she decided, Liberace would certainly be a big star someday. The crowd's enthusiasm and acceptance

The New Frontier about the time Elvis and Liberace were performing here

portended nothing short of fame. An astute businesswoman, she upped his salary to $1,500 after that first performance.

Audiences adored Liberace, and word soon got around town. The Last Frontier was not the only establishment willing to hire him. Years later, Liberace would tell the story about the night that Bugsy Siegel came to make him an offer of employment. Everyone in town knew who Siegel was. They also knew that no one told him no. But that is exactly what Liberace wanted to do. How could he refuse gracefully, and still continue breathing? A few days later, the problem was solved by Bugsy's murder.

As his popularity grew, Liberace continued to enjoy salary increases. By 1972 he was commanding $300,000 a year at the Hilton Hotel. His fans came from all walks of life, and from all over the world. Blue-haired grannies and long-haired teens were counted among his adoring fans. Nowhere did he have more fans than in Las Vegas. There are still many people in town who remember his kindness and his culinary skills.

Of Liberace, one person who attended some of his dinner

parties says, "Yes there was Gladys [the cook], but Lee was also a wonderful cook. He never seemed happier than when he was preparing a special meal for his friends. His personality was completely different than his stage persona."

Las Vegas will never forget Mr. Showmanship. Apparently this is the way he wanted it. Rumor is that he still haunts some of his favorite Sin City places.

Vegas Villa

Outward appearances can be deceptive. Located a short distance from the Liberace Museum and Carluccio's is a middle-class neighborhood of modest older tract homes. It is not the sort of neighborhood where you might expect to find the former residence of a Las Vegas megastar. But Liberace lived here for many years. The home at 4982 Shirley Avenue is actually two houses that were converted into a fabulous showplace fit for Mr. Showmanship.

Money was no object; Liberace filled his home with priceless objets d'art and specially designed furnishings. From its exterior, the home seems ordinary; inside, it is pure star, complete with ostentatious trappings. Mirrors and marble abound. From the main front door an ornate staircase leads to the entertainer's favorite room. The room is less formal than the rest of the house. Its hues are dark. If not for the skylights it would be almost somber. Filled with expensive trinkets, the room's walls are covered with $200,000 worth of imported Moroccan tile that shimmers in the steamy Las Vegas sun.

There are bubble baths, and then there are bubble baths. Many years ago a magazine did a photo spread of Liberace's digs that featured the pianist himself, reposing amidst a million bubbles in his one-of-a-kind bathtub. And what a bathtub it is.

While the lavish marble master bathroom is as large as most people's living rooms, it is the pillared sunken $65,000 bathtub surrounded by etched mirrors and two-thousand-year-old Grecian marble pillars that is the room's centerpiece. And what better lighting than the exquisite $25,000 Baccarat Crystal chandelier that hangs overhead.

As one of Las Vegas's highest paid superstars, Liberace could afford to indulge his every whim. After a visit to the Vatican City and the Sistine Chapel, he decided that he had to have just such an exquisite ceiling for his bedroom. To make his dream a reality, Liberace hired a descendant of Michelangelo to paint a replica of the Sistine Chapel on the ceiling of the master bedroom. The work is valued at well over a million dollars, but who can put a price tag on a dream? Certainly Liberace couldn't.

Across from the master bedroom was his mother's bedroom. No expense was spared when it came to mama either. With a walk-in closet that could easily house the entire wardrobe of a Hollywood screen star, the room is ordinary by comparison. Mama preferred the slot machines to lavish surroundings. When she became so old that Liberace worried for her safety and comfort, he did what any doting son would do. He applied for, and received, one of only two private gambling licenses in the state of Nevada. Thus duly licensed, he purchased a slot machine for mama's enjoyment and had it installed in the Shirley Street home. There she could wile away the hours in the comfort of her famous son's home.

Those who wish to take a peek at such grandeur will be happy to know that weddings and other special events can be booked at Las Vegas Villa. Apparently the ghostly Liberace drops in at his former residence from time to time. A member of a wedding reception held at the villa insisted he had seen Liberace hovering near his piano.

"My mother was a fan. I know what the man looked like. And I'm telling you that I saw his ghost. He was a foot or so off the floor and just sort of floating in midair. He saw me looking at him and smiled sweetly. I turned to see if anyone else was aware of him. When I turned back, he was gone."

The following incident was related by a woman who toured the villa recently:

I was standing a yard or so from the water fountain in the foyer where all the mirrors are. I noticed a stream of silvery blue water spiraling down from the ceiling. As I watched the water cascade to the floor, I told myself to be very careful not to slip in the small puddle that was forming. Then I started wondering how the water could be coming from the ceiling. I didn't see any tubes or water pipes connected to the water fountain. What on earth was leaking, I wondered.

I looked up where the stream of water had been, but it was gone. The floor was dry; there was no puddle or any indication that it had ever been wet. Something told me to look up again, and so I did. That's when saw the blue painting of Liberace's face on the ceiling. I got chills down my back when I realized it was exactly where the stream of water had come from!

Liberace enthralled his audiences with his musical genius and his outlandish stage attire: the more sequins, feathers, and flash, the better. Like the fans of Elvis, Liberace's followers adored him. He was indeed Mr. Showmanship; Las Vegas embraced him and claimed him as its own. For his part, Liberace loved Las Vegas. Perhaps this is the reason he stays on.

Redd Foxx

John Elroy Sanford (yes, that was his real name) came to Las Vegas during the early 1950s. It was a time when African Americans were not even welcome to stay in the high-class hotel/casinos. Entertainers like Lena Horne and Sammy Davis Jr. might be drawing paying customers to the gaming establishments, yet they were consigned to the Westside of town. In time, Sammy Davis Jr., Frank Sinatra, and others would help to right this terrible wrong.

But Sanford was a man who did not give up so easily. He had lived with racial prejudice most of his life, and it would not deter him. He knew that his talent would eventually take him all the way to the top. Until that time, he lived by his wry wit. There was no middle ground for Sanford;

audiences either hated his routine, thinking it vulgar, or they loved every minute of it.

Once success was assured, Sanford took the stage name Redd Foxx, and quickly became the mainstay of casinos eager to entertain their guests. As a testament to his star status, he built a home, complete with swimming pool, on Eastern Avenue. There he settled in to live the good life, Las Vegas style: casino hopping and gambling. A Vegas old-timer remembers seeing Redd in the Keno lounge at various casinos. "He could be the nicest guy you ever want to meet, and generous. Or foul mouthed and rude. It just depended on how his luck was going that night."

And as his fame continued to rise, his career and his good luck were assured. Television execs were watching. Ever on the lookout for fresh new talent, they agreed that Redd Foxx would be perfect, if they could clean up his act. There were no foul-mouthed, four-letter words permitted on television at that time.

A deal was struck, the contract was signed, and in 1972 Foxx slid into the role of the cantankerous Fred Sanford on the aptly titled TV series *Sanford and Son.* Just as execs had predicted, audiences adored the star, and the show was a hit. But as sometimes happens in the entertainment industry, personalities clashed. Problems between Foxx and the show's executives mounted and could not be resolved. Eventually Foxx and the show parted ways. He wasn't concerned. After all, he was on top. He could find another show. In the meantime the IRS got tired of waiting for the bundle of back taxes they claimed Redd owed them.

There was nothing for them to do but take Redd's home at 5460 South Eastern Avenue; in doing so, they summarily tossed Foxx out on his ear. Bitter at the way he had been treated, Redd recovered and continued to look for another television job. It came in 1991 when he went to work on *The Royal Family,* a new weekly series that costarred his dear friend Della Reese. For a time it looked as if things had finally turned around for the comedian. The IRS was off his back, and things were looking up. On October 11, 1991, one month after the first episode of his new show aired, Redd Foxx grabbed his chest and toppled over on the set. Sadly some of those present thought it was just another of the comedian's jokes; he was dead of a massive heart attack.

Shortly after his death the IRS put Redd's home up for sale. It sold quickly, and the new owner moved in. Almost immediately strange things began to happen. There were the unexplained cold breezes. Try as he might, the owner could find no obvious reasons for the drafts. Then the doors and windows began to open and close on their own. An early morning sighting of a ghostly Redd Foxx convinced the new owner that the home was indeed haunted by the comedian. He had been a fan of Foxx's, but the knowledge that his ghost was still in residence prompted the man to sell the home and move out.

The home's next owner was a commercial business. After a hasty renovation the business moved in and opened its doors. All went well, until Foxx's ghost began appearing before startled employees. One woman said, "I think he meant to tell me something. He walked right up like he was going to speak to me, then turned and was gone."

Apparently Foxx's favorite room was his former bedroom. Here is where he most often appeared. He was also spotted walking down the hallway or outdoors by the swimming pool. Employees continued to be perplexed by items that moved of their own volition, and doors that opened and closed on their own. Sensing that Foxx meant only to outmaneuver the IRS and to stay in residence, no one was afraid of the ghostly comedian. Eventually the business moved out, and another renovation took place.

Las Vegas Paranormal Investigations, under the direction of Mike Carrico, have been permitted to investigate the home a few times. Aside from a misty anomaly in one of Mike's digital photographs, electronic voice phenomena, or EVP, have also been captured in the building. Before the swimming pool was filled in, investigators heard unseen people laughing and talking in the pool house area out in the back of the building.

Shannon Day Realty now occupies Foxx's former home. They had a tiny red fox painted on their mailbox in honor of the building's original owner. Perhaps, some say, this gesture may even serve to appease the spirit of Redd Foxx.

It's not enough to induce the ghostly comedian to move on. Redd still loves Las Vegas. And prankster that he is, Redd gets a kick out of teasing the ladies. Occasionally employees will hear someone walk through the lobby. When they go to greet the visitor, they discover no one there. It's only Redd, the wily Foxx, up to his old tricks.

Elvis Presley

Las Vegas is a city of Elvis impersonators. Look around at the showrooms, laundromats, supermarkets, and wedding chapels; Elvis look-alikes are everywhere. It wasn't always so . . .

Elvis made his Las Vegas debut in the spring of 1956. Billed as the Atomic Powered Singer, the twenty-one-year-old performed nightly in the Venus Room of the New Frontier Hotel. As an added attraction to the Freddy Martin show, Elvis's appearance was heralded as a Las Vegas scoop and one of the most lavish productions the New Frontier had ever offered. And yet, he was not a hit.

There was no label to pin on his style. He was considered an oddball with his itchy-twitchy gyrations, waterfall hair, and blue suede shoes. In a series of publicity shots, he and fellow entertainer Liberace attempted to stir up some interest by switching jackets and instruments, and hamming it up to the delight of news photographers. Yawn; no one else seemed to notice.

Elvis's music appealed to rebellious teenagers, but it did nothing for their parents, the people who spent money in Vegas, where cash counts. He just couldn't grab the interest of the more sophisticated showroom-going crowd. And so the Atomic Powered Singer bombed.

After a stint in the Army, he starred in a string of Hollywood films like *G. I. Blues, Blue Hawaii,* and *Viva Las Vegas.* Under the tutelage of his manager, Colonel Tom Parker, the former heartthrob continued to hone his style. One day he would draw Las Vegas audiences.

In 1967 Elvis and his girlfriend, Priscilla Beaulieu, arrived in town like thousands of other starry-eyed couples and prepared for a wedding. After a brief eight-minute ceremony at the Aladdin, Elvis and Priscilla were husband and wife. As the bride and groom duly cut into the six-tier white wedding cake, photographers happily snapped their photos. Fans were delighted. They adored the stylish new Mrs. Presley with her heavily teased bouffant hairdo, and Queen-of the-Nile eye makeup. What they really loved, however, were the changes in Elvis.

More than a decade had passed since he had swiveled onto the *Ed Sullivan Show.* He was older and richer, had several movies to his credit, and seemed to be in the process of changing his look even further. He was no longer sporting his luxurious black sideburns.

By the early 1970s, Elvis and Priscilla had gone their separate ways. He was living in the fast lane of excess. Plump and out of shape, he cavorted on stage in a skintight sequined jumpsuit and cape. According to one rumor, his girth was managed by a specially designed girdle. Who cared? He had a retinue of adoring fans. Many of the teenage girls who had swooned over his first film, *Love Me Tender,* were now middle-aged matrons with long memories and husbands with fat wallets, who were also Elvis fans. And they were more than willing to shell out the ticket price for the chance to remember how it was back in the day. These were the people he sang to, the people he tossed colorful scarves at, his most devoted fans.

His performances at the International Hotel (later the Hilton) set Sin City records that few entertainers would dare attempt to match. During the seven years from 1969 to 1976, Elvis performed 837 consecutive sold-out shows before two and half million people. That's $43.7 million spent for tickets to see Elvis. And that's a hunka hunka lotta cash.

He was on top. There was nothing left to strive for. He had achieved it all, and his abuse of prescription drugs and his overeating continued. Then in August 1977 Elvis's world came crashing down around him. He was the King, he was forty-two years old, and he was dead. All the King's medics, and all the King's money, couldn't breathe life back into the cold form on the floor of the master bathroom at Graceland.

Elvis couldn't be dead! James Dean be damned, stars aren't supposed to die. We don't want our icons moldering in their graves. Then came the hoax theory; he was alive out there somewhere. Elvis had wanted to shirk his fame and live the good life. He was wandering the globe in happy anonymity. True enough, Elvis was spotted everywhere, from Bakersfield to Bangkok.

One way or the other, the King had to be kept alive if only in our hearts; for that to happen it would take his fans' undying devotion. It would take the hopes and dreams of those who wanted to be like him, sing like him, speak like him, and most of all, be adored like him. While he was alive, his look was good for little more than a party joke, a Halloween costume. Now that he was gone, Las Vegas latched onto the King in earnest.

From all across the country, Elvis impersonators descended on the city. Some came in shades and outlandish wigs, others in white stretch jumpsuits sparkling with dime-store spangles. All wanted their share of the glory that had been his. Some grew weary of waiting and went back home. Others stuck it out, knowing as long as the Elvis image sold, there would be work. The ghostly Elvis wasn't having any of it. He might have died in Memphis, but he promptly returned to Las Vegas. He is the King, after all.

A year after his death, the Hilton honored Elvis with a bronze statue. On hand for the celebration and the unveiling ceremony were his father Vernon and his ex-wife Priscilla. The statue, which bears little resemblance to

Elvis, has been moved several times since then. Today you will find it in the Hilton lobby.

Ghost hunters in search of the spectral Elvis may want a photo with the statue, but they should look elsewhere for the King. For starters there is the Elvis Suite on the thirtieth floor. Elvis usually stayed here whenever he was in town. Some insist that his spirit still haunts the luxurious suite. Others believe he is in the wings of the Hilton showroom. Just as he had been spotted in points across the globe, the ghost of Elvis began turning up in the backstage areas of some local showrooms, particularly that of the Hilton Hotel, shortly after his death. This apparition is Elvis the elder, plump and attired in the trademark jumpsuit. He is said to hand out sweat-stained scarves and then vanish in the night. Other witnesses claim that he stands silently brooding in the wings a moment, and then he is gone . . .

Says one person, "Go ahead and call me crazy if you like. But I saw the ghost of Elvis, big as you please. I was working the graveyard shift at the time. I was polishing the floor about three in the morning when something just made me look up. That's when I saw him coming across the hall. At first I thought it was one of the impersonators . . . and then he just disappeared right there in front of me."

One of the most famous people to have seen the apparition of Elvis is singer and longtime Las Vegan, Wayne Newton. In his 1989 autobiography *Once Before I Go,* Newton tells of seeing the ghostly Elvis sitting in the balcony during one of his performances.

Apparently, Elvis's ghost gets around the globe and around Las Vegas. His apparition has been seen at the fabulous Hartland Mansion, one of Las Vegas's swankiest wedding and reception locations. Think oooh-la-la elegance and glamour. So what was Elvis doing here? He was rumored to have been a guest at the Hartland from time to time, while performing at the International Hotel.

Harder to explain is the occasional sighting of the ghostly, and decidedly younger, Elvis at the Landmark

Drug, where he once filled up on his prescriptions. By the time Elvis had the need to frequent this pharmacy he was older and out of shape. Perhaps the King prefers looking younger and vibrant. Don't we all!

Some researchers of the paranormal believe that excessive grief or admiration can keep a spirit from making the necessary transition after death; like an anchor or a chain these strong emotions hold the spirit earthbound. Given the adulation that he has received since his untimely death, it would not be too surprising then for Elvis to stay on.

Elvis may have left the building, ladies and gentlemen, but apparently he hasn't left Las Vegas.

Elvis Séance on a Rainy Afternoon

It was August 16, 2004, the twenty-seventh anniversary of Elvis's death. Storm clouds gathered over Sin City, and a séance was planned in his honor. A curious group gathered in the showroom of a local casino on this dreary afternoon and waited to see just what might happen.

Many of them had never been to a séance, and didn't know quite what to expect. Maybe the King himself would deign to appear before them. Would he wear his sequined jumpsuit or jeans and leather jacket? Perhaps a pair of blue suede shoes would suddenly materialize and tap out time with the old Elvis tunes that played softly in the background. Love me tender, wouldn't that be something?

All eyes were on medium/illusionist Dixie Dooley as he stepped onto the stage. The table was set with spirit-calling paraphernalia: bell, candle, chalk, tambourine, etc. And so it began, this séance that would summon the dearly departed Elvis.

"Elvis," Dooley began. "We know how much you loved Las Vegas. You performed right across the street. Are you here with us today?"

Silence.

Members of the audience squirmed in their seats. Surely

Elvis would offer some sort of sign to those loyal enough to his memory to come out in this weather.

"Elvis!" Dooley coaxed sweetly. "If you're here with us this afternoon, please give us a sign."

No sooner were the words out of Dooley's mouth than a thunderclap roared across the sky; suddenly rain started pelting the roof.

"It's a sign!" a woman exclaimed. "He's here!"

"Maybe so," Dixie cautioned.

As rain continued falling, the roof sprang a leak. This was turning out to be one wet and unusual day in the desert. The séance was concluded. A top-notch stage manager could not have timed the thunderclap any better. Was it Elvis or merely a coincidence? Some walked out into the pouring rain convinced that the King had heeded Dixie Dooley's call, stepped across the hereafter, and given them a thundering sign of his return.

Love him tender; love him true, later some would recall that a similar rain had fallen on the night Elvis died.

Frank Sinatra and the Rat Pack

They were five guys who liked to have a good time. They were the Rat Pack: Frank Sinatra, Sammy Davis Jr., Peter Lawford, Joey Bishop, and Dean Martin. During the 1950s and the 1960s they were the coolest cats this side of the galaxy. And they were regulars in the Copa Room at the Sands. Dressed in expensive threads, they drank, chain-smoked, and kept the casino's patrons entertained with their songs and good-natured, if sometimes naughty, repartee. It was all good. And all good for the bottom line, not to mention the fact that Sinatra owned a small percentage of the Sands.

In 1960 Las Vegas was abuzz; the Rat Pack was in town and working on a new film. *Ocean's 11* is the story of a group of men who carry out a daring plan to rip off five Las Vegas casinos on New Year's Eve: the Sands, the Desert Inn, the Riviera, the Sahara, and the Flamingo.

It's a small world, especially in Las Vegas. Coincidentally,

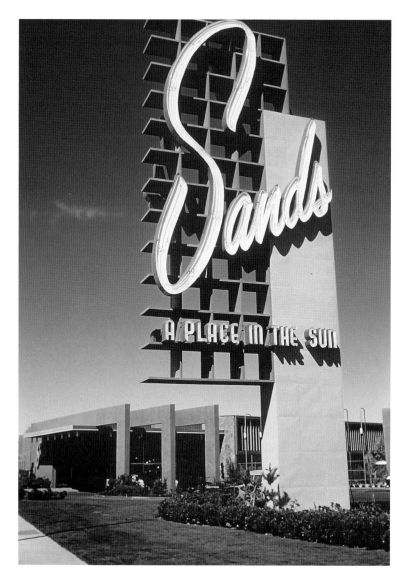

The Sands when the Rat Pack appeared here

one of those making a cameo appearance in the film was George Raft, who had been an actor pal of Benjamin "Bugsy" Siegel. Now that's a kick in the head! The film was a quickie that took only twenty-five days of shooting.

Nonetheless, *Ocean's 11* was well received. Despite its outdated hairstyles, clothing, and slang, it still wears well, even today, and even in comparison to the George Clooney et al. remake. The Rat Pack would make more movies, *Sergeants 3, 4 for Texas,* and *Robin and the 7 Hoods,* but none would be successful, or capture the moviegoers' imaginations the way *Ocean's 11* had.

In 1960 *Ocean's 11* was at the theaters, and Las Vegas and the Rat Pack were more popular than ever. That same year John F. Kennedy defeated Richard M. Nixon and was elected to the presidency. Kennedy was in the White House, and members of the Rat Pack suddenly found themselves with political connections; Peter Lawford was, after all, the brother-in-law of the President of the United States. And the pack, especially Frank Sinatra, didn't mind boasting about their "in" with the movers and shakers.

This was a more innocent time. It would be decades before the public became aware of Kennedy's womanizing and his supposed affairs with Marilyn Monroe and Judith Exner, a paramour of mobster Sam Giancana. The Rat Pack had its connections, convoluted or not.

Giancana would figure prominently in the Nevada Gaming Control Board's revocation of Frank Sinatra's gaming license. Listed in the board's black book of those undesirables barred entrance to Nevada gaming establishments, Giancana visited Sinatra's Cal-Neva Lodge in the summer of 1963. That visit was well documented, and it eventually cost Sinatra not only the Cal-Neva Lodge, but also his percentage of ownership in the Sands.

But nothing lasts forever, especially in Las Vegas. The city loved Sinatra. Mayor Hank Thornley presented a Proclamation of Appreciation to him in 1970, and in 1981 his gaming license was reinstated; it probably didn't hurt that one of his character witnesses was none other than President Ronald Reagan. Oh, those presidential connections.

And while we are on the subject of presidential connections, at his passing, Ronald Reagan was given one of Sin City's highest honors when the lights of The Strip dimmed momentarily in remembrance. This honor was also shared by Rat Pack members Sammy Davis Jr., Dean Martin, and Frank Sinatra, the man who did it his way.

Apparently Old Blue Eyes is still doing it his way in the afterlife; the entertainer is believed to haunt both the Cal-Neva at Lake Tahoe and the Golden Nugget in Las Vegas. According to former employees of the Cal-Neva, Sinatra has been spotted numerous times in his showroom. A few years ago a Golden Nugget cocktail waitress nearly dropped her tray of drinks when she saw Frank walk through the pit and vanish like a stranger in the night. Sensitive Chris Fleming also encountered Sinatra while filming a segment of his British television series, *Dead Famous.*

Frank Sinatra and the Rat Pack are long gone. For that matter, so is the Las Vegas they once knew and loved. But you can't help but wonder if the group doesn't occasionally sally forth and hold court in some little out of the way joint known only to them.

And the Women Ghosts . . .

So that's it for the men. Now what about the women? Sorry to say, there aren't any famous female stars haunting Sin City: no Marilyn Monroe, no Jayne Mansfield, and no Bette Davis. Not that they didn't spend some time here. A decade before she hit the big time, the future Marilyn came to Las Vegas seeking a divorce. Still Norma Jean, she shed her spouse and hurried back to Los Angeles, stardom, and a new moniker. Occasionally Marilyn hung out here with Frank Sinatra and the Rat Pack. One rumor has her planning to do a big Las Vegas extravaganza show, shortly before her death.

She would have been following in the footsteps of fellow blonde bombshell Jayne Mansfield. During her foray into the Vegas showroom circuit, Ms. Mansfield performed in a specially designed shimmering see-through dress before packed houses at the Tropicana and the Dunes. Casino big shots were delighted. For her titillating services, the well-endowed star was pulling down a hefty weekly salary that was more than the President of the United States was earning.

That is what being popular in Las Vegas will get you—that and maybe a street named after you. Roll the dice and change the scenario. The show went to hell, and Ms. Mansfield ended up in smaller venues with a likewise smaller paycheck. There is no Jayne Mansfield Street yet, but there is Frank Sinatra Drive and Betty Davis Street. Note the spelling on the latter; it's not exactly how Ms. Davis spelled her first name, but then again, it's the thought that counts. There is also Debbie Reynolds Drive, but there aren't any ghosts on Debbie Reynolds Drive, unless you count the ghosts of marriages past.

When Eddie Fisher dumped Debbie Reynolds for her good friend Elizabeth Taylor, he headed off to Las Vegas for his six weeks residency and quickie Nevada divorce. The plan was simple; the two lovebirds would be wed as soon as Debbie was shed.

While Mr. Fisher and Ms. Taylor awaited their nuptial bliss, he headlined at the Tropicana, and she sometimes sat near the stage swooning. How romantic is that? Kiss, kiss, and have a slice of wedding cake. Too bad their marriage was as ill fated as his and the discarded Debbie's had been. But that was a long time ago, a very long time ago in Vegas years. No doubt, all has been forgiven and forgotten . . .

Meanwhile back on Debbie Reynolds Drive, let's talk tacky. Jayne Mansfield was dead and buried when the Fremont Hotel sent her a bill for seven thousand-plus dollars for costumes. So although the fame that stars achieve may be interred with them, sometimes their debts live on after them.

Take heart; there may not be any famous women haunting Sin City, but there just may be a ghostly showgirl or two.

Ghostly Showgirl

Showgirls are statuesque and self-assured. Men fantasize about them. Women envy them. But their work is grueling, and their careers are short-lived. Even in the hands of the most skilled plastic surgeon, no one can hang on to beauty and youth forever. Gravity takes its toll, and endurance fades. And honestly, who really wants to still be strutting across a stage wearing a scattering of sequins, a hot pink-feathered headdress, and little else at age fifty?

When a Las Vegas showgirl had the misfortune of being murdered in her apartment, no one realized that she might decide to stick around for a while . . .

Decades later when another young woman moved into an older apartment complex, her thoughts on ghostly activity were ambivalent. It didn't take long for her to discover that she was sharing her home with a ghost.

From the day she moved in, she had an unshakeable feeling that she was never really alone in the little four-room unit. She had heard the stories about a showgirl being strangled in the apartment. Supposedly the murder happened in the 1960s; she doubted it would have any effect on her life. Besides that, for all she knew there was no truth to the story.

But after a while she began to notice that her hairbrush and makeup were often misplaced, and she found her books and magazines in the oddest places. She assured herself it was merely forgetfulness. When her perfume began to smell like an entirely different fragrance, she blamed it on her allergies.

And then came the morning when halfway through her shift, she suddenly became so ill she had to go home early.

I was so sick it's a wonder I was able to drive home. When I got there, I practically crawled into my apartment. I barely had the strength to throw myself on the sofa. I lay there on the sofa a little while, and then I heard what sounded like humming in the bedroom. My first thought was that I had left the radio on. I listened a few minutes and went in to turn it off.

That's when I saw her sitting at the foot of the bed; she stared into the mirror and applied lipstick. A feeling of sadness rushed over me . . . She was nearly transparent and seemed to be glowing; I knew she wasn't real. My heart was thumping. I forgot all about being sick. I told myself she must be the murdered showgirl and summoned up all my courage.

Somehow I knew what had to be said. I spoke softly: "I know it was a terrible thing that happened to you. But that was a long time ago, and you can't stay here any longer. You don't belong here anymore. It's time for you to move on."

She turned, smiled at me, and quickly vanished . . . It's odd, but she must have listened to me. I never saw or heard her again. And nothing was ever again misplaced.

As we all learned from *Fried Green Tomatoes,* a lady always knows when to leave.

Chapter 4

Guns and Ghosts

Today's hotel/casino megaresorts are operated by corporations whose accountants keep an eye on the profit margin. Both the state of Nevada and the federal government oversee the industry with a long list of rules and regulations that must be adhered to; this is where the attorneys come in.

Someone needs to help translate all this legalese for the casino employees who work in the gaming end of an operation. And it is a very serious business. Heavy fines, jail time, and the loss of one's gaming license are the result of violating gaming regulations. No one wants to go there.

Back in the day, things were different. Mobsters ran their operations safe in the knowledge that the rules did not apply to them. Everyone in town was hip to the fact. The Dunes, the Sands, and the Stardust all had underworld affiliations. What did you expect? Gaming was a lucrative business all right, and anything went, just as long as there was enough cash to skim off the top.

Benjamin "Bugsy" Siegel

The city of Las Vegas may have been incorporated a year before he was born, but anyone can tell you that the father of modern Las Vegas is none other than Benjamin "Bugsy" Siegel. He did not breathe his last here, but this is the city he loved. And that makes the handsome gangster one of Sin City's most famous ghosts. The dapper Siegel would probably have liked all the attention, even as much as he despised the moniker Bugsy.

Benjamin Siegel was born to impoverished immigrant parents in a New York tenement on February 20, 1906. While others went about their lives oblivious to the starkness that surrounded them, Bugsy did not. He wanted to rise above the poverty any way he could. His way was crime. As a teenager, he met Meyer Lansky, and a lifelong friendship was forged. Together, the two streetwise young men formed what would be known as Murder, Inc., a gang of thugs who took what they wanted, even when it called for maiming, or killing, anyone who stood in their way.

Over the years Siegel and Lansky grew close; each trusted the other more than they should have. When personnel problems started mounting in Los Angeles, Meyer Lansky didn't think twice. He would have to do something or lose his stronghold out West. And Lansky wasn't one to lose. So he sent his pal Siegel to straighten things out. Bugsy swaggered into Southern California and quickly fell under its spell. Before long he was soaking up sunshine during the day and squiring beautiful starlets all over Hollywood by night. It didn't long for him to realize that this is where he wanted to stay. There was no way he could go back to the East Coast after hobnobbing with Hollywood's elite.

With his good looks and charm, Bugsy played the role of a single man about town, effortlessly forgetting about the wife and children waiting back home in New York. Accustomed to breaking the rules, he rented a spacious home in Beverly Hills and moved the family out to California. Nevertheless, he continued his pursuit of several leading ladies. When things got too boring in Los Angeles, Bugsy and his current girlfriend would head for a little rest and relaxation in the desert gambling town of Las Vegas, some 275 miles east.

Bugsy was fascinated by Nevada's legalized gambling. One night while nursing his drink, he noticed how much money customers were losing, and how easily the house raked it all in. Everyone was happy, even the losers. Legalized gambling, he decided, could make a man very rich. And he wanted to be in on it. Here were all these people chasing after a winning hand, and not scared of losing, or raising their stakes.

Nevada knew what it was doing, all right. These suckers were willing to risk it all at the tables, the roulette wheels, and the slots. And they would come back again and again, just for the chance of winning. He may have had only an eighth-grade education, but Bugsy was smart enough to figure the odds. And those were always in favor of the house.

Siegel had come to Vegas to oversee Lansky's horserace betting operation when he first began to seriously consider the potential here in the desert. There were a few gambling establishments like the El Rancho and the Last Frontier, but Las Vegas still lagged behind Reno as gambling's fun spot. The forty-year-old city had seen its shot at fame come

Early day Las Vegas

and go with the Boulder Dam Project. Now Vegas needed a new direction. And Benjamin Siegel, he reasoned, was just the man to see that it happened.

There was a tremendous amount of money to be made here for the right person. And amazingly, it was all legal. No one had to rob anyone. The suckers couldn't wait to hand over their cash. They called it gambling, but Bugsy knew better. He was nobody's fool; sooner or later the house wins. Always!

So while he oversaw the interests of Lansky, Siegel made his plans. Meanwhile out on Highway 91 a restaurateur, publisher, and gambler by the name of Billy Wilkerson kept busy watching his dream take shape in the form of a highbrow gambling establishment. He was ready to show these cowboys a thing or two about class. Black-tie evening attire was the order of the day. There would be no rowdy, casually dressed, kick-ass cowboys in his place—unless they were sweeping the floors or washing the dishes. Even then, they would be required to exchange the boots and blue jeans for high-class uniforms.

Wilkerson ran a swank restaurant in Hollywood. He liked rubbing elbows with the stars. But stars got bored easily. They were always on the lookout for the next thrill. In Vegas he could give that to them by offering fine dining and games of chance. All he had to do was build a classy enough place, and Hollywood's elite would come scurrying across those two hundred-plus miles of desert, bringing with them lots of cash. Classy, that's what Wilkerson wanted his establishment to be.

Like Wilkerson, Siegel admired class. The moment he set eyes on what the restaurateur was building, Bugsy realized it was the gold mine he had been dreaming of. It mattered little that Wilkerson owned the property; Siegel wanted it. And in true Bugsy fashion, he shoved Wilkerson out of his dream and into an agreement. A legal document was quickly drawn up. Ever the gambler, Wilkerson figured the odds and gladly signed on the dotted line. After all, signing away his dream was better than taking up permanent residence in a six-foot plot of the Southern Nevada desert. There were no dreams there.

Now that Siegel was in charge, and the hotel was on its way to becoming a reality, he renamed it. The hotel would be known as the Flamingo in honor of, some said, his long-legged girlfriend Virginia Hill. For her part, Virginia could have cared less about the hotel's name, just as long as the easy money rolled in.

The town was sizzling with excitement. World War II was over, and jobs were plentiful. But not everyone agreed with Bugsy about the Flamingo. On August 1, 1946, the *Las Vegas Tribune* carried a front-page editorial criticizing him for having the audacity to use scarce material in the building of a casino. According to the editorial, this material could be put to better use by building homes for returning war veterans—especially since the Civilian Production Administration (CPA) was organized for the purpose of building homes rather than commercial establishments.

Bugsy knew how to get what he wanted. Regardless of the methods he used in securing them, he obtained his building permits from the Civilian Production Administration, and construction of the Flamingo continued. While he held tight to his bosses' purse strings, the cost of scarce materials rose. Everything he needed was overpriced, and then there were the delays and the thefts. An old Las Vegas story involves workers stealing material in the evening, only to redeliver and recharge for it the very next day. Bugsy would probably have killed anyone he caught cheating him in such a scheme. But he was none the wiser.

Eventually his lack of attention would cost him dearly; he would pay for the cost overruns with his life. The estimated cost of building the Flamingo was 1.5 million dollars; it wound up costing six million dollars. He might have been an excellent gangster, but Siegel was no businessman.

After patiently waiting for him to stop his philandering, Bugsy's wife finally decided enough was enough and left for Reno where she filed for divorce. Now Bugsy had more time to pursue Virginia Hill, the new woman in his life. Virginia was beautiful and vivacious and liked to spend money. It didn't matter whose money she spent.

It is a widely held belief that Bugsy was murdered because he and Virginia lived the high life on cash skimmed from his employers. Even so, the thefts might not have been so unforgivable had the Flamingo turned a profit early on. But luck was against Bugsy.

It was opening night, December 1946, and finally, at a cost of over five million dollars, the Flamingo was officially open for business. It was wintertime in Las Vegas. A freak storm had hit the West Coast in full force. As heavy wind-driven rain washed across the valley, Jimmy Durante, Rose Marie, and other top-name entertainers attempted to please the sparse crowd of gamblers who had bravely come out in the pouring rain to see what the Flamingo and Bugsy were all about.

Just as Billy Wilkerson had envisioned, the Western Cowpoke look of the other Las Vegas establishments was

Bugsy's dream casino

missing. The décor was modern up-to-the minute swank; class as interpreted by Benjamin Siegel. No bolo ties, boots, blue jeans, or plaid shirts. Bugsy and his staff were attired in formal wear. It may have seemed a bit pretentious to those accustomed to the El Rancho Vegas and its casual Cowboy Western theme. But no one dared say a word as Bugsy in white tux greeted his guests warmly. He was especially eager for the money to start rolling in and the bottom line to turn from red to black.

He hadn't figured all the angles; the hotel was not finished. When customers grew weary of gambling, they had no choice but to leave the premises, taking all their money with them. To make matters worse, the crowd was much smaller than he had anticipated. Two hundred and seventy five miles away in Los Angeles would-be patrons were kept away because of a raging winter storm that had grounded all planes. This was not at all the way Bugsy's dream was supposed to unfold.

Eventually the Flamingo would become a huge moneymaking success. Unfortunately, Bugsy would not be around to bask in the glory of being proven right. On this night his bosses watched anxiously as the crowds dwindled. Their fury mounted. They had squandered enough money in the Nevada desert. All hope of quickly recouping their losses was dashed. And everything was blamed on Bugsy Siegel. If he hadn't been too busy chasing after Virginia Hill, he might have kept a better eye on their interests. Then too, some of them believed that Bugsy and Virginia were helping themselves to the bosses' cash. This belief and the dismal opening night take put Bugsy on a crash course with destiny. No one could save him, not even his longtime friend Meyer Lansky.

The end came for Bugsy on June 20, 1947. He never saw it coming. He had prepared for violence in Las Vegas by surrounding himself with a retinue of bodyguards. His penthouse at the Flamingo was locked behind a steel-reinforced door and bulletproof windows. Concealed in his closet was a secret escape ladder that led down to an awaiting getaway car in the garage tunnel that could take him to safety in the eventuality . . .

At 810 Linden Street stood Virginia Hill's rented Beverly Hills home. Virginia was traveling in Europe. Later, opinions would differ as to whether she had been out of town by accident, luck, or design. The heat hung in the air. Darkness had fallen, but it was one of those Los Angeles summer nights that would take hours to cool down.

Bugsy and his friend returned from their early dinner and settled onto the sofa. He casually glanced at his newspaper and switched on a reading lamp. There was plenty of time. He knew that eventually a companionable silence would fall between them. Then he would read the paper. Their conversation was idle, old-friend chitchat, punctuated by laughter.

The killers silently crept up the long driveway to the mansion. Theirs was a job that required stealth and cunning. They watched and waited. The flowered drapes had not been drawn. A bright light illuminated the entire room. The target was in full view, relaxed and unaware of what fate had decreed. They took aim . . . Three shots rang out in quick succession . . . There was nothing left of Bugsy but a shattered bloody corpse slumped on the colorful chintz sofa.

Panicked houseguests came running. The acrid smell of blood and death filled the room. Within minutes the police would come, and the photographers and the reporters. As Bugsy cooled under a white sheet on a steel gurney at the Los Angeles coroner's office, a swift change of management was underway at his beloved Flamingo. He was dead and gone, but the world and the Flamingo Hotel were moving on.

At his funeral only five mourners gathered to see him off to his final resting place. Across the desert, it was business as usual in Las Vegas. Gamblers eagerly tossed their money into the Flamingo's coffers while the new management kept a close eye on the bottom line. Benjamin "Bugsy" Siegel was yesterday's news.

In time no one would forget him. Bugsy's vision paved

the way for Southern Nevada's hotel/casino industry, and in celebration of its fiftieth anniversary, the Flamingo remembered him by putting his likeness on its five-dollar chips. Several items pertaining to Bugsy are on display at the Nevada Historical Society located in Lorenzi Park. Included in the display are photos of the Flamingo, the door to Siegel's penthouse, a chandelier from the penthouse, the agreement signed between him and Billy Wilkerson, and a scissors set. Bugsy would be especially pleased to know that there's not a Bugsy in the bunch; everything is labeled as having belonged to Benjamin Siegel.

Bugsy was slain in Beverly Hills, yet his apparition was regularly spotted in his penthouse suite at the Flamingo. Then came the day in 1996 when progress took its toll, and the building was razed. With his penthouse lying in rubbles, the ghostly gangster was forced to find other digs. So he began hanging out at the Flamingo's rose garden where a monument bears his likeness and an inscription covers his ownership of the hotel. An Iowa couple told of seeing the ghostly Bugsy just outside the rose garden wedding chapel one summer night.

"We saw him over by the fountain and thought he was one of the Bugsy tour guides the way he was dressed. It was around ten at night and still almost a hundred degrees. We felt sorry for him having to wear that shirt, tie, and wool jacket. As other people started coming up to the fountain no one seemed to notice him. Then this woman walked right through him . . . It was the scariest thing we ever saw. I don't think the woman even saw him. She was posing for a picture, and smiling . . . No, I'm sure she didn't see him."

Ghosts are not necessarily consigned to the places of their death. If they are of free will and able to go to the spots they enjoyed in life, it stands to reason that Bugsy would seek out the Flamingo where his dream first took shape.

Riding Alongside Bugsy

Virginia Ridgway knows about ghosts. As the curator of

the world-famous Goldfield Hotel, she encountered more than her share of visitors from the other side of the grave. A hands-on healer, and a sensitive, Ridgway appeared on countless television shows that cover the paranormal. If you have ever watched *Scariest Places on Earth, Dead Famous,* or *Ghost Adventures: A Raw Documentary into the Paranormal,* you've seen this adorable senior lady in action.

When not involved in one of her Nevada tourism projects Virginia loved to travel, especially with her daughter, whenever she had the opportunity. On this particular vacation, they were in Las Vegas and doing the town up right. Staying in one of the poshest of the posh suites at a local hotel/casino, the two women decided to take friend Robert Allen's Haunted Vegas tour. They boarded the bus and found themselves chatting with a friendly man who happened to be alone. As Virginia told the story . . .

He got on the bus and sat directly across from us. He was alone, and I guess he decided we would keep him company. Every time the guide cracked a joke, our new friend laughed louder than anyone. I thought he might have had one too many drinks; otherwise, he seemed perfectly all right. Robert's tour is always fun. Everyone was enjoying themselves, especially our new friend. The strangest thing occurred when we got to Bugsy's garden at the Flamingo Hotel.

I noticed that he seemed very interested in what the guide had to say about Bugsy Siegel. He even chuckled and said the guide was wrong a few times. We got off the bus, and he was right behind us, laughing and talking as we walked through Bugsy's garden and on over to the memorial. I turned around to ask what he thought of the monument, but he was gone. The guide thought he might have gone to the restroom, and waited five minutes for him to return. He never did.

Finally the bus left without him. I asked the guide where he thought the man might have gone, but he was as dumbfounded as we were. He said it was the first time anything like that had ever happened. Someone asked me if I thought the mysterious man might have been Bugsy's ghost. He could have been.

Bugsy Ghost Hunt

It's a given. When ghost hunters get together, they go hunting for ghosts. Since Benjamin "Bugsy" Siegel happens to be one of Las Vegas's favorite spirits, the rose garden

Bugsy memorial in the rose garden of the Flamingo

and Bugsy memorial at the Flamingo was chosen as the Las Vegas Paranormal Conference's ghost investigation site.

Ghost investigators hopped off the bus with dowsing rods, cameras, recorders, and other ghost hunting equipment, and headed their separate ways. Every one of them hoped to make contact with the man who started it all, or as one man said, "Bugsy is probably the coolest ghost goin'."

Yeah, but watch that Bugsy stuff, won't you? If the ghostly gangster is anywhere within hearing distance, he's probably not too happy with that nickname.

Photographers remarked that there were orbs everywhere: by the memorial, the fountain, and the wedding chapel. Nowadays many ghost investigators discount orbs as dust particles, bugs, moisture, and just anything but paranormal. It didn't matter. Some in this group were positive that at least one of the orbs was Bugsy, come to communicate.

The recorders are on. "Bugsy . . . Uh, I mean Mr. Siegel, are you here with us tonight?"

A pair of dowsing rods pointed toward the wedding chapel. "This is where he is seen," the dowser said excitedly. Psychics were wary. None felt the presence of the ghostly gangster. And other than the shaking rods, the orbs, and some whispered EVP there was no sign that Bugsy had made an appearance in the rose garden that night.

Gus Got His

Bugsy Siegel's pal Gus Greenbaum may be among the ghosts who haunt the sites where long-ago Las Vegas casinos once stood. Bugsy's bullet-ridden body was barely cold when Gus grabbed the reigns of the Fabulous Flamingo. If he was nervous about his predecessor's fate, Greenbaum kept it to himself. He was from way back; the mobster could take care of himself. And so he did. With a little help from his gangster buddies, Greenbaum pulled the Flamingo out of the red. For the first time in its existence, the Flamingo was showing a profit, to the tune of four million dollars. Not bad, Gus. From there he went on to manage the Riviera. But shades of Bugsy, Greenbaum developed a taste for the high life.

When he started skimming to cover the high cost of drugs, gambling, and women, his bosses took a dim view of his management style. As with all such hits, Gus was miles from the Las Vegas city limits when it came. Relaxing at his Arizona home with his wife, Gus looked up just as the killers walked in. It was the wrong time, wrong place for the missus; her throat and his were slit from ear to ear. It was all quiet and effective. The moral? Simple: don't steal from the bosses.

Bonnie and Clyde

No, Depression-era bank robbers turned murderers, Bonnie Parker and Clyde Barrow, never made it to within five hundred miles of Las Vegas. Before they ever had the chance to consider the merits of a slot machine, the cold-blooded duo was dispatched from this world in a merciless hail of bullets near Sailes, Louisiana, in the early morning hours of May 23, 1934.

Times were tough. Bonnie and Clyde were tougher. Some wondered if they were really dead. Anyone who doubted the effectiveness of the lawmen's bullets could gawk at one postmortem photo after another. One shows Bonnie, black and white, bloated and sans makeup. Another presents Clyde, full of bullet holes and staring. After the public's insatiable curiosity was satisfied with several gruesome photos, they concurred: the pair was as dead as dead could be. There was nothing left to do but bury them and forget them; ashes to ashes and dust to dust. And so their bodies were taken home to Dallas, Texas, and buried. Yes, it was the end for Bonnie and Clyde, but unlike Bonnie's prediction in her poem, they do not repose side by side.

If not for Las Vegas and its propensity for quirkiness, this is where the tale of Bonnie and Clyde might have ended. But the rusted-out, bullet-ridden car that took the lawless pair on their ride into eternity is on display, in all its gory glory, at the Primm Fashion Mall. And if that is not enough to lure tourists and satisfy anyone's morbid curiosity, there is also the faded blue shirt Clyde was wearing when the bullets ripped into him. If anything can be gathered by peering through the glass case at the old shirt, it's that Clyde was a rather small man. A letter from a relative, who probably sold the shirt for more money than Bonnie and Clyde ever stole from a bank, attests to its authenticity.

Also on display are several rare Barrow family photographs, a mirror, a belt, and assorted pieces of jewelry Clyde created while cooling his heels in prison. These items meant a lot to Clyde in life. Perhaps they do in death as well.

The deaths of the nefarious twosome certainly qualify as sudden and unexpected. It could be that the spirits of Bonnie and Clyde are somehow attached to this car, unaware that they came to the end of the road more than seventy years ago. Ask the employees if there are any reports of the car being haunted, and see how fast they tell you no.

However, there are those who have worked on the car up close and personal, and they will tell you something very different. Sightings of ghostly people sitting in the infamous auto, and feelings of foreboding and terror when near the car, are a few of the stories associated with the Bonnie and Clyde car. Given the extent of violence, this isn't surprising.

At one time people were free to touch the car to their heart's content; today it is surrounded by a glass enclosure. A man who visited the car several years ago told the following story about it:

> I was a kid at the time, and we had come to Las Vegas to visit my grandparents. We were just coming through Jean [Nevada] when it started to rain. Dad pulled off at the mall, and we decided to go in and look around.
>
> When we saw the car my dad started to tell me all about Bonnie and Clyde and led me up to it. I never will forget

this as long as I live. I reached out and touched the car, and when I did, I heard the most terrible screaming and crying. I almost wretched at the smell that surrounded me, but when I took my hand off the car it was gone. No one had heard the sounds I did. My folks said it was imagination playing tricks on me, but I don't think so.

During the Las Vegas Paranormal Conference, mediums Deborah Senger and Paula Schermerhorn, called the Mystik Koz, visited the Bonnie and Clyde car. As they stood staring at the vehicle Deborah suddenly gasped. "There's a man in the back seat. He is pounding on the rear window trying to get out."

While they all looked at the empty car, a bystander told Deborah, "There was a third person in that car. I feel that you just witnessed his horror when he realized he was about to die."

Senger is not alone in what she saw that afternoon. Others have also seen the ghostly man desperately trying to get out of the Bonnie and Clyde car. Who he is and why he is riding into the hereafter with the two killers is anybody's guess.

Tony Cornero Shoots Craps at the Desert Inn

Before the Desert Inn was demolished to make room for the Wynn Las Vegas, Howard Hughes was rumored to be haunting one of the penthouse suites. Down in the casino a dapper little man was occasionally spotted at the crap table—the ghost of an old mob man who died here back in the day, they said. Anyone who saw him didn't want to talk about it. No one wanted to admit that they might have seen the specter of the long dead Tony Cornero.

Bugsy showed them the way. After his abrupt departure from the Vegas scene the mob continued to tighten its grip on many of the larger casinos. Two-bit crooks slipped into town, in hopes of scoring a big bankroll and ruling the roost. Some succeeded. Others, like Tony Cornero, only dreamed of success. And Tony's dream was ambitious. He wanted to build the world's largest hotel/casino on The Strip and call it the Stardust. It wasn't as foolhardy as it sounded. Cornero was not new to the ins and outs of gambling; he had run gambling operations like the Meadows and the Rex. His ability to raise venture cash was legendary. No one in Vegas could raise money faster than he could.

Along the way, construction costs overran Tony's bankroll. Tapped out, he made nice and borrowed enough cash from Bugsy's old pal Meyer Lansky to keep his Stardust dream alive. Too bad Cornero couldn't do the same for himself.

Everyone in Vegas knew that Tony loved to gamble. His favorite casino was the Desert Inn, or D.I., as locals referred to it. So there was Tony, at the D.I. on a hot July morning in 1955, a big shot shooting craps, when suddenly—hold all bets—the Grim Reaper grabbed him.

It was a heart attack, they said, and the body was swiftly taken to a back room far from the paying customers' prying eyes. Seven years earlier a gunman had attempted to kill Tony when he opened the door of his Beverly Hills home. This time he was a goner. While Cornero's corpse cooled, Las Vegas tongues wagged. Someone had popped Tony. It was so slick, the killers would get away clean. Neither the sheriff, nor the coroner was notified for several hours after the demise. In that time, according to rumor, Tony's cocktail was dumped down the drain. And his glass was washed till it sparkled. The whisper was that a fast-acting poison had killed Tony. If so, no traces would ever be discovered. But who was looking? No autopsy was ever performed on the body of Tony Cornero. Happily, however, work on the Stardust Hotel continued on schedule. Priorities!

Tony the Ant: Tony Spilotro

In this city of wedding chapels, one is reputedly haunted by gangster Tony Spilotro. It seems that Spilotro ran a business at the location, and, rumor has it, may have even murdered a couple of detractors there as well. If the wedding chapel is haunted, who is doing the haunting? Is it the ghostly Tony, or one of his victims? One thing is certain. When Spilotro died, he died like Benjamin "Bugsy" Siegel and Gus Greenbaum: violently and miles from Las Vegas.

Tony Spilotro swaggered into town in 1971, sent to oversee his mob bosses' interests. He bought the gift shop at the Circus Circus for $70,000 and proceeded to play the big shot—a big shot with two very distinct sides. Tony the Ant was courteous to the casino's hired help, but he could be ruthless with those his bosses held in disfavor. Spilotro didn't negotiate. It was far too easy to beat someone into his way of thinking. Or kill them if they stood in the way of his and his bosses' plans.

Surprisingly, some retired service workers remember Spilotro as being kindhearted and generous. Apparently he wasn't stingy when it came to tossing a couple of dollars to the waitresses and the busboys. Gratuities are always appreciated, nowhere more so than in Las Vegas, where they are called tokes. This is a city that lives and dies by its tokes. A good toke can sometimes mean the difference between eating and going without. Las Vegans, who work in the service industry, depend on those tokes. Tony Spilotro realized this fact better than his crooked cronies did.

A retired waitress, who waited on him numerous times at a hotel/casino that has long since been imploded, said:

> We knew him as Mr. Stuart. So Mr. Stuart it was. He was always nice to me . . . always left me a good toke. When he was with a group of people and soon as they finished their meal, he would ask them, "What about the girl? Did you leave her a tip?" If they didn't answer him, he would ask me, "Honey, did they get you?"
>
> I knew who he was. Everyone in town did. And I knew who they were too. So I just smiled and said, "Yes sir."
>
> Even if they hadn't left me a nickel . . . It was terrible what happened to him and his brother. Terrible! No one

deserves to die like that . . . All I can say is, he was always nice to me.

But there was that other side of Anthony Spilotro, the side nobody wanted to see; those who did see it, didn't live to tell about it. So what if the mob had its hands in several of the casinos' cash vaults. It was a fact that Las Vegans lived with, like taxes and death, you might say. No one liked it, but they learned to live with it.

When the Circus Circus tossed Tony out on his ear, he sold his gift shop at an unbelievable profit and moved on to the Dunes. There it was business as usual, until Tony got greedy. He was getting his share, but still, seeing all that money his bosses were raking in must have really riled the ant.

So he hired several handpicked thugs and set about in his own moneymaking scheme. You can talk about small-town gossips all you want. Nothing moves swifter than the gossip of Las Vegas. When Tony's bosses got wind of what he was up to, they were furious. You might make time with the boss's wife and live to tell about, maybe. But when you get greedy, start making deals behind his back, and cheating him out of his money, your days are numbered. His favor was gone; he was nothing but a liability. And he had to be dealt with.

Tony and his brother Michael were summoned for a special meeting. None the wiser, they hopped a plane and headed eastward, business as usual. Only it wasn't. Tony probably didn't see it coming any more than Bugsy and Gus had. Like them, he was far from the glitter of Las Vegas when karma kicked in. He and his brother were savagely beaten to death in an Enos, Indiana cornfield. Has Tony the Ant returned to haunt Las Vegas or does his apparition wander through that cornfield trying to figure out how he went wrong?

Someone who wasn't impressed with Spilotro's generosity laughs. "It's pure and simple. Tony crossed the wrong people. So what if he left good tokes all around. Good tokes don't mean jack when it comes to getting whacked in a cornfield."

Obviously not!

Wilbur Clark's Desert Inn as it appeared when the mob ruled Vegas

Pitching Cards at the D. I.

Back in the day Wilbur Clark was the Desert Inn's front man, the man whose face was seen on all the matchbooks and other casino advertising. He was the man everyone naturally assumed owned the joint. Not true. While building the Desert Inn in 1947, Wilbur ran out of money. In order to keep the project alive, he did what most businessmen do; he took on partners. Beyond looking at their bankroll, he didn't ask questions. Later he informed the Kefauver Investigation that he hadn't realized he was partnering up with men who had mob connections.

The following is from a time when the Desert Inn was booming. Tony Cornero had bitten the dust, and Howard Hughes had not yet moved in. Blackjack dealers, or twenty-one dealers, if you prefer, have one of the toughest jobs in the casinos. Their job is to stand in the pit and pitch cards to casino patrons. Seems easy enough. It's not! Dealing cards requires concentration, and personality, and a thick skin. This is especially true when an irate customer resorts to verbal insults after losing hand after hand, or a pit boss starts sweating another customer's big winning streak. Either way, the dealer generally bears the brunt of the anger.

Unflinching concentration is crucial. No doubt this

is why blackjack dealers are accorded regular twenty-minute breaks throughout their shifts. Forty minutes on, twenty minutes off, just enough time to grab a sandwich, have a smoke, go to the restroom, or visit with fellow dealers. Generally considered the elite in casino hierarchy, blackjack dealers customarily sit with each other.

One Saturday night the dealers had plenty to talk about. Within an hour of one another two tourists toppled off their high-backed chairs. They were dead before they hit the carpet was the general consensus. No one likes to talk about customers who die in the casinos; it's bad for business. And what's bad for business is just plain bad. The paramedics rushed in and whisked the unfortunate men out ASAP.

They were assumed to be gone and forgotten. Then Rusty (not her real name), a redhead who had dealt cards at the Desert Inn for more years than she cared to remember, saw one of the men standing right there at her table. Looking forlorn and confused, the specter turned and vanished as quickly as he had appeared. She knew what she had seen, but was wise enough to keep it to herself. Within a week of her sighting, Rusty overheard another dealer talking about seeing the ghost walk through the pit. She kept silent, but the others continued to talk.

Pit bosses hear it all; what they don't hear, they see. Like other members of casino management, they are sometimes referred to as "the suits." And like other members of management, the pit bosses keep an eye and an ear on the casino's best interests. Before long the whispers made their way to the ears of Rusty's pit boss, and he was furious.

What if customers heard the story? It could dampen the enthusiasm of especially superstitious players. Then too, they might go elsewhere to gamble, God forbid! Think of the bottom line. The hush was on. No more talk of a ghost in the pit. Occasionally Rusty would see the ghostly gent standing at her table, but thankfully he never pulled up a chair and placed a bet.

You Never Know . . .

When you rent a place, you don't really know what happened there a week ago, a year ago, or decades ago. You may live in a brand new house, condo, or apartment yet sometimes have the strangest feeling that your abode is haunted. It's possible. Your home may be twenty-first-century new, but the land it sits upon is as old as the earth itself. What weird things occurred on that land or in the area a hundred years ago? Or even fifty years ago? Is it possible that the remnants of some tragic event played out decades ago still lingers? Do the ghosts of those who discovered too late that tempting fate is seldom wise haunt certain places? The following stories are not of mobsters and hardened criminals but people who broke the law and regretted it, one way or the other.

Death-defying Dive

At an ultramodern apartment building that has long since given way to progress, a young man attempted to defy the odds. He knew it was against the rules. But he couldn't resist showing off. And diving into the shimmering swimming pool from the balcony of his second-floor apartment was something he was mighty proud of. In fact, he was so proud of his successful dive that he jumped out of the pool, ran back up the stairs, and stunned onlookers for the second time with another flawless swan dive.

As any gambler knows, luck can change in an instant. Instead of walking away the winner in his weird game of chance, the daring young man stood poised on the balcony set to dive into the pool for the third time. But this time his luck ran out; he miscalculated the distance and was killed instantly when he dived headfirst onto the cement of the swimming pool area . . .

A Shot in the Dark

Okay, maybe all of those old black-and-white sitcoms

in which everything turned out right in thirty minutes or less were a lot of hokey. Nonetheless the world did live by a more rigid code of conduct during the 1950s. It was a man's world. Despite Mamie Eisenhower with her straight as sticks bangs and white-glove inspection tours of the White House, and Marilyn Monroe with her little girl voice and larger than life bustline, it was still a man's world. Men ruled the roost, and women wanted to be Grace Kelly and marry the rich prince from Monaco. While ruling the roost, men were expected to be gentlemen, and women, dreaming of Prince Charming, were to be ladies, no matter what. But some marched to a different drummer.

She was a waitress at one of the local eateries. He was a card dealer at the Horseshoe. They were adults, divorced, and lonely. When they met, it was by chance. He stopped in for a quick meal before heading home to his lonely apartment, and gave her the once-over. Flattered, she responded in kind. Within the week they were dating. They discovered that they had a lot in common, and the romance blossomed. A month later they were meeting at the home he had once shared with his ex-wife.

Soon they fell into a routine. They drank, made love, and drank some more; on occasion they quarreled. Their arguments were nothing serious, certainly not like the acrimonious battles they had shared with their long-gone spouses. Until the night she really made him mad.

Her words were knives that cut into his fragile ego. Naked or not, she had to be locked out of the house. This was Las Vegas. It wasn't that cold. He shoved her out the back door and bolted it shut. Smugly silent, he listened at the door as she pleaded with him to let her in or at least toss out her clothes. She could beg all she wanted. He wasn't about to do either. His ex-wife might have warned her that he hung onto his anger longer than most; her ex-husband might have warned him that she was relentless when it came to getting her own way.

After a few minutes of silence he wondered if she had

given up. She hadn't. However, she had remembered something. There was a gun in the glove compartment of the friend's car she had borrowed. She skulked out to the car and returned to the door with the weapon.

Thinking that the gun would be just as good a key as anything else, she took aim at the lock and fired. Unfortunately her erstwhile lover had chosen that very moment to listen at the door; the bullet struck him just below the heart. He was dead, and she would later be arrested on a charge of involuntary manslaughter. Propriety first and foremost, she was properly attired when the first police officer arrived on the scene.

Chapter 5

Las Vegas Early Days

Glamour, excitement, sunshine (there are more sunny days here than there are in Florida), opportunity, and a sense of being part of a city that is truly phenomenal, this is what Las Vegas is all about. The city is relatively new; it is the only major American city to come into being during the twentieth century. And yet this one-of-a-kind city, Nevada's largest, was actually part of Arizona Territory until Nevada's state boundary was rearranged in 1867. It was Nevada's gain to be sure!

It's easy to get sucked into the illusion that Vegas is all new: the razzle-dazzle light displays, the replicas of the Statue of Liberty, the Eiffel tower, and a Venetian gondola ride, plus of course the stars. Yeah, here you can rub shoulders with the men and women who pull down megasalaries for starring roles in the movies and on weekly television—that is, if you party at the swank places and aren't afraid of betting big bucks with the best of them.

All new also are the slick stretch limos and the women with lollipop-colored hair and bodies that Mother Nature never intended them to have. Don't be fooled. The city may be new. But Las Vegas is an old place, a very old place . . .

Ghosts of the Kiel Ranch

Time and eager real estate developers have swept away most of the old Kiel Ranch. The city of North Las Vegas has grown and slowly encroached upon the thousands of acres that were once part of the largest ranch in the area. Located in the industrial section of North Las Vegas, the old Kiel Ranch is a shadow of what it once was. After a 1992 fire destroyed most of the old buildings, all that remains of the ranch is a large lot surrounded by a padlocked chain-link fence.

Locked behind the fence are thick patches of drought-resistant weeds, scattered debris, the burned-out replica of a ranch house, and the old adobe, which is the oldest structure in the Las Vegas area. The prelude to the Las Vegas area's first mystery was played out here on a long-ago July morning. Perhaps no one will ever know the truth of that day, except for the lonely ghosts who still roam this desolate area.

As a kid, he remembered playing here among the tall grass and ramshackle houses that were once the Kiel Ranch. That was back in the 1950s before the city was a megametropolis of high-rise casino/resorts and traffic jams. Back in the day . . .

If our parents didn't come and pull us home we would stay out there playing ball till way after dark. No harm done. There wasn't anything here that we could break. It had all been broken a long time ago. My brother and I were usually the last to leave. Our mom and dad worked swing shift. There was no one at home to make us go indoors after dark. Believe me, we really took advantage of that.

After all the other kids left we were tossing the ball back and forth when these two men walked out from behind the old Kiel ranch house. I stopped throwing the ball and stared at them. My brother saw me staring and asked what I was looking at. I pointed to the men, but he didn't see them. The men were scared. I could tell by the way one of them pushed his hat up off his forehead and the way they kept looking back over their shoulders. Their fear scared me, but at the same time, I somehow knew they weren't real. For one thing, my brother couldn't see them.

When they got up closer to where I was standing I could see they were sort of glowing, and their eyes were blank, like they were dead or something. That was enough for me.

I grabbed my brother, and we ran outta there fast as we could. I don't know who they were. Or why they were there that night. But I do know they were a couple of ghosts.

When talking about a haunting, some paranormal researchers will compare a ghostly haunting to that of a place memory. A place memory haunting does not involve an interactive ghost at all, but rather an incident, usually traumatic, looping itself over and over in time. Think of a scene from a movie repeating again and again, sort of like what happened to Bill Murray in *Groundhog Day*. The murders of Archibald Stewart and the Kiel brothers were never solved. That these three murders were somehow connected, there can be little doubt.

Justice was not served. The killers of these men lived out their lives never having to answer for what they had done here at the Kiel Ranch. This could just as easily give rise to a ghostly haunting or a place memory.

Death of the Kiel Brothers

It was October 11, 1900. Fierce winds swept across the Las Vegas Valley bringing the promise of fall and its respite, however brief, from the heat that shortened men's tempers and shriveled crops still on the vine.

In a coincidence that boggles the mind and seems to flout the laws of probability, Archibald Stewart's son Hiram and his foreman went to the Kiel Ranch to visit and do business with their neighbors Edwin and William Kiel, the sons of Conrad Kiel. The older Kiel had been dead many years. With his passing the bitterness between the two families had seemingly ended.

Strange that the sound of approaching horses had brought no one from the ranch house to greet the visitors. It was the neighborly thing to do. But they knew full well that the two Kiel brothers didn't always do the neighborly thing. The men dismounted and knocked on the door. When no one answered their knock, they waited a moment then stepped inside the house, calling to its occupants. Something wasn't right here; it was too quiet. They glanced toward the kitchen and discovered Edwin's lifeless body sprawled across the floor; a gunshot wound to the head had cut short his stay on this earth.

The men cautiously backed out the door and started looking for William, the other Kiel brother. The search ended when they found him nearly submerged in the irrigation ditch some yards from the house. Whatever had happened here at the Kiel Ranch, it hadn't been pretty. William's injuries appeared to be more substantial than those of his brother: a shotgun wound in the left arm, a second in the chest, and a third bullet lodged near the left eye.

A coroner's jury later determined that Edwin had killed William in a fit of rage; then, they surmised, he became filled with remorse at what he had done, and turned the gun on himself. Of the thirty or so people who lived in the Las Vegas Valley at that time, some wondered if perhaps Hiram Stewart hadn't taken revenge on the Kiel brothers for his father's untimely death. Just as that of Archibald Stewart had been sixteen years earlier, the deaths of the Kiel brothers would remain shrouded in mystery.

Edwin and William were buried in wooden coffins beside their father in the family cemetery on the Kiel Ranch. The truth of their deaths seemed destined to be just one more in a string of mysteries. Then, in 1975 came an opportunity to discover some answers in the case of the three deaths. The body of Archibald Stewart was to be exhumed at the site of the old Las Vegas Ranch as the city of North Las Vegas began to expand.

In a world whose resources are continually being depleted, progress must sometimes make way for the living at the expense of the dead; after all, the dead don't pay taxes, and they don't vote.

So the old cemetery was excavated and the bodies removed. Forensic experts at the University of Nevada-

Las Vegas Anthropology Department set to work and soon discovered that Archibald Stewart was felled by two different weapons. This bears out statements that were made by those who had seen his body shortly before burial. In the case, Kiel brother Edwin was vindicated. Another interesting finding was the fact that the angle of William's wounds indicated there might have been more than one killer at the Kiel Ranch.

What was the reason behind the cold-blooded killing of the Kiel brothers? Who had murdered them? Could their killings have been in retaliation for that of Archibald Stewart?

Some of those who played as kids near the old Kiel Ranch when there were empty lots all around have told of strange noises and fleeting sights caught in an instant out of the corner of an eye. Could this have been a glimpse of the ghostly Archibald Stewart in the final moments of his life, or the restless spirits of the Kiel brothers as they faced their ghostly assailants?

All three men are said to haunt the old Kiel Ranch area. A ghostly man has been seen running across the area where the old ranch house once stood, and there have also been reports of strange noises in the area.

This is the place of three violent and unexpected deaths. One thing is apparent: the killers of the Kiel brothers managed to escape justice, and if Archibald Stewart was killed, not in self-defense, but in cold blood, his killers also managed to escape the law. Perhaps the ghosts of Kiel Ranch want merely to right old wrongs.

Boulderado

The Kiel Ranch would have several names and owners in the years following the Kiel brothers' mysterious deaths. A divorce dude ranch called Boulderado was probably the most popular. With the much-publicized 1939 Clark Gable/Rhea Langham divorce, the Las Vegas divorce trade came into its own. By 1940 more Hollywood celebrities were choosing Las Vegas over Reno to sever their matrimonial ties. As the city successfully wrested its share of Nevada's divorce-seekers from the Biggest Little City up north, another need became apparent. The stampede of divorce-seekers would need a place to spend their required six-week residencies.

The sweet smell of money was in the air. A group of astute businessmen bought the Kiel Ranch and converted it into the Boulderado Dude Ranch. News spread. And here they came, the hottest celebrities of the day, to soothe their bruised egos, to soak up some sun, and to mingle. And there was always the possibility of another matrimonial hookup.

Perhaps one of the lonely ghosts that walk the old Kiel Ranch is not Conrad Kiel, his unfortunate sons, or Archibald Stewart, but a man who came here long afterward seeking a divorce. If so, someone should tell him that his six weeks residency has long since passed.

The Old Mormon Fort

A replica of the old Mormon Fort is located on North Las Vegas Boulevard at Washington Avenue. It was on this spot that the city of Las Vegas began. Among the interesting items at the old fort are the first flag that flew over Las Vegas, farming and household implements, and family photographs of Helen and Archibald Stewart.

Weary travelers stopped at the Las Vegas Ranch for water, rest, and refreshment before moving on to their destinations. The Old Mormon Fort is all that remains of those long-ago days. A trickle of water snakes its way past shade trees and clumps of grass and rocks. Don't be fooled. Like many of Las Vegas's attractions, the creek is a replica; the area's ever-increasing demand for water long ago sucked the original creek dry.

When Brigham Young sent his faithful out from Utah in 1855 to settle the farthest reaches of the territory, William Bringhurst, brought thirty Mormon missionaries to this region. They set to work and eagerly built a fort that was little more than an adobe-walled enclosure. Within this enclosure they planted their crops that were irrigated by water from the creek and the nearby springs.

The crops flourished. But the blistering desert heat proved too much for the settlers. After only two years, they abandoned the site. If not for modern air-conditioning few could comfortably live here in the Las Vegas Valley on the edge of the Mojave Desert.

In 1865 Octavius D. Gass purchased the land and proceeded to build the large Las Vegas Ranch. When his crops failed, Gass found himself facing money worries for the first time since he had taken over the ranch. There was nothing to do but make two loans with Pioche rancher Archibald Stewart. As collateral, he put up the Las Vegas Ranch. At 2½ percent interest per month, the loans were a heavy financial load for the rancher to carry. Sixteen years later he defaulted on both loans and lost the property to Stewart.

As soon as the title was his, Archibald Stewart packed up his family and left Pioche. When he moved onto the ranch, Gass's friends were outraged. Stewart made no pretense of being friendly with his neighbors, and was despised throughout the valley. Those who murdered him must have been disappointed when they realized that his widow was not about to sell. Under her direction the ranch would remain in the Stewart family for several more years.

Then in 1902 Helen Steward, with uncanny foresight, sold the land and the water rights to the San Pedro, Los Angeles and Salt Lake Railroad. Mrs. Helen Steward would continue to live in the city and to play an important part in early-day Las Vegas. Today she is known as the First Lady of Las Vegas.

Ghost Hunt at Old Mormon Fort

If there's even the slightest hint that a location is haunted, ghost investigators want to check it out. The Old

Mormon Fort is such a place. Local ghost hunters have conducted impromptu investigations at the site of the old fort for a number of years. While none of these have produced earth-shattering evidence, some have left the investigators convinced that the place is haunted.

At least one ghost is said to walk the grounds of the old ranch late at night. Those who have seen him describe him as gaunt. The phantom is usually spotted near the site of the old ranch house, or at the replica of the pioneer garden. "He darts about as if he were in a hurry," said one witness. "It almost seems like he is running late."

Maybe this is the ghostly Archibald Stewart still overseeing his ranch as he searches for justice. Not all ghostly sightings are of men. The following took place at the old fort years ago.

> It was a gray day, windy and cold with heavy clouds blocking out the sun. I was just leaving the fort when I happened to see this woman walking through the pioneer garden. She was wearing a long dark-colored dress and lifted the skirt up as she moved along the cacti. When she noticed that I was watching her, she seemed uncomfortable.
>
> "Looks like rain," I said, trying to ease her discomfort.
>
> "Perhaps," she snapped and walked right into thin air.

Spring Mountain Ranch

During his buying frenzy, Howard Hughes wasn't just buying up every hotel/casino he could get his mitts on. The eccentric moneybags also bought himself a working cattle ranch fifteen miles west of Las Vegas, the Spring Mountain Ranch. In doing so, Hughes was taking control of one of the oldest sites in the Las Vegas Valley. Buildings at the ranch are the second oldest in the Vegas area.

Long before Howard came with his checkbook, Native Americans visited this site within Red Rock Canyon for its more than fifty springs. As early as the 1830s, long before Mormon settlers, Conrad Kiel, Octavius Gass, and Archibald Stewart arrived in the Las Vegas Valley, explorers taking an alternate route of the Spanish Trail were camping here. Wagon trains would continue passing through the area right up to the time that the railroads came to Las Vegas in 1905.

In 1876 James B. Wilson and his partner George Anderson filed a claim on five hundred acres at the base of the Wilson Cliffs. They would call their ranch the Sand Stone Ranch. The two men worked the ranch until Anderson pulled up stakes, leaving it and his two sons in the care of Wilson. This was the last they would see of Anderson.

Wilson raised the two boys as his own, giving them his name; when he died in 1906 they inherited the ranch. Over the years, the ranch changed hands several times. Aside from Hughes, actress Vera Krupp, wife of German war criminal, industrialist Alfred Krupp, was its wealthiest owner. Krupp bought her ranch in 1955 for a million dollars and changed its name to the Spring Mountain Ranch.

Vera, who had once invested in the New Frontier Hotel and Casino, dug her tiny cowboy boots in. She was here to stay, and would reside at the ranch longer than any other owner. However, once Vera was back in Vegas and settled into ranch life, she wanted her freedom. So she sued Alfred, back in Germany, for a divorce and millions. As a convicted war criminal Alfred was barred from entering the United States. Even if he had wanted to keep the lovely Vera, he could not come to Vegas to plead his case. Vera prevailed.

To make herself comfortable, the wealthy divorcée did some remodeling at the ranch. A wing was added to the ranch house and a swimming pool added to the grounds. If she needed cheering up, Vera had her trinkets. One of them was a 33.6-carat diamond believed to carry a curse. Indeed it had not been very lucky for her ex-husband Alfred; six months after gifting Vera with the stone, she bid him *auf Wiedersehen.*

Her affection for Alfred may have turned cold, but Vera

adored her diamond. Now dubbed the Krupp diamond, she wore it wherever she went. While picking up supplies in Vegas, Vera wore her standard ranch hand getup (jeans and Western shirt), and on her finger was the sizeable sparkler. The diamond caught the eye of a crook by the name of George Reves. Reves did the math; he knew the rock was worth a lot of dough. So he plotted with others of his ilk to steal it.

On April 11, 1959, Vera and her foreman were relaxing with drinks when someone knocked at the door. Thinking it was a crew to blacktop the driveway, Vera opened the door. It was Reves and his pals, all armed with guns. The men shoved their way into the ranch house and tied up Vera and the foreman. After viciously tearing Vera's prized diamond from her finger, the crooks ransacked her house. When they left they took the Krupp diamond and several other pieces of jewelry with them.

After freeing themselves, Vera and her foreman discovered that the ranch phone was dead. To report the robbery they had to drive to the Vegas airport. Eventually the diamond and Reves were found in Elizabeth, New Jersey. Reves went to prison, and the diamond was returned to Vera. After her death in 1967 Richard Burton bought the Krupp diamond for Elizabeth Taylor, who owns it still.

With the robbery fresh in her mind, Vera took precautions. A secret bedroom and passageway were built in the ranch house. To get into the room, someone would have to go through her closet. As time passed, Vera grew less content on her 520-acre ranch. She offered to sell it to the U.S. government for use as a park. Nothing doing. The million dollar-plus price tag was too steep.

In stepped Howard Hughes and his checkbook. Hughes bought the ranch from Vera six months before she died at the age of fifty-seven.

When salivating developers purchased the ranch with plans to build condos and faux ranches for the deep-pocketed set, the public balked. More streets, cars, pollution, and infrastructure were just what Las Vegas didn't need. Why should the wealthy be the only ones to enjoy every inch of picturesque land that nature ever created? This time, someone was listening. Thanks to their efforts, today the ranch is part of the Spring Mountain Ranch Park in the Red Rock Canyon National Conservation Area. Many of the original buildings survive, as does the old Wilson family cemetery. It is open to the public, and tours are available.

Fifteen miles from Las Vegas, but a world apart, things are totally different. At the foot of the Wilson Range, where the ranch is located, the views are breathtaking. No wonder Vera Krupp, Howard Hughes, and previous ranch owners loved the place so. But the question remains: Is Spring Mountain Ranch haunted? Some believe it is. To get a better idea the Las Vegas Paranormal Investigations conducted an investigation at the park recently. Their tools included voice recorders and cameras. The focus of the investigation was the old school building, the cemetery, and the Wilson cabin. At each site, the investigators were able to capture EVP.

Visitors at the ranch house can ogle Vera's closet and some of her finery. Not only was she an elegantly attired lady, but a very, very lucky lady as well. Imagine owning all this only a few years after having worked as a salesclerk in a department store. Some believe the ghost of petite blonde Vera remains here at the ranch. Others cast a suspicious eye out toward the old Wilson family cemetery. Are there ghosts at Spring Mountain Ranch? When asked that question, a docent said he had heard the stories, but didn't want to get any rumors started.

Nelson and the Techatticup Mining Camp

Even before the Spaniards came to Eldorado Canyon in search of gold, ancient Anasazi and later Paiute Indians called this place home. With the California Gold Rush, rich ore was on everyone's mind. In 1859 came news of the big silver discovery in Virginia City. About that same time, mining began here in earnest with the discovery of rich gold veins. The Techatticup Mine was formed in the 1870s and continued producing for the next seventy years. In that time more than 250 million dollars in gold, silver, and ore were taken from the mine.

Today only about thirty people live here in Nelson, some forty-five miles south of Las Vegas. At one time there were more people living here in Eldorado Canyon than were in the Vegas Valley. That was a long time ago, when thieves and murderers roamed the canyon. Today ghosts roam the Techatticup.

One of them is Charlie Nelson, for whom the town is named. Charlie never knew what hit him. He was murdered by Avote, a Paiute who was not happy with the white men's coming to the region and set about to rid the canyon of as many as he could. Avote continued his killing spree until the white men demanded that something be done. As was the Paiute custom, the duty of bringing his murderous relative to justice fell to Avote's brother, Queho.

After tracking him for several hours, Queho met up with Avote on Cottonwood Island. There was nothing to do but execute the wrongdoer. And so Queho shot Avote. To prove that the sentence had been carried out, he cut off his brother's hand and returned it to the white men. Another version of this story has Queho cutting off Avote's head and carrying it back to Nelson in a burlap bag. Either way, the ghostly Avote is said to walk the canyon to this day, searching for his head or his hand. Take your pick.

Some claim that Avote was not a murderer, but a convenient scapegoat behind whom the real killer hid. If that is the case, you can certainly see why Avote hangs out here in Eldorado Canyon.

The sun is down, the campfire is lit. If you think you hear howling coyotes, listen carefully. Those may not be coyotes at all, but the canyon's famed hell dogs. These ghostly canines are said to roam the area, snarling and howling their unhappiness. Don't get too close, they just might bite.

The Mystery of Queho

Queho was born about the same time that the infamous Mouse of the Valley of Fire met his fate. Like Mouse, there would be many different stories told about him. The only common thread running through all these tales is bad luck. Queho was an orphan; he would never know his parents. His mother died shortly after giving him birth, and the identity of his father remains a mystery. He was raised by his mother's relatives at the reservation in Las Vegas and was not accepted by the others.

In the superstitious world in which he lived, a deformity was considered a bad omen. Some stories claim it was Queho's clubfoot that set him apart and made him an outcast. Others say his right leg was noticeably shorter than his left. Either way, he grew up resentful of those who treated him badly.

Queho was the stepbrother of outlaw Paiute Avote. According to legend, which may or may not be an exaggeration, Queho turned to the same crimes as his brother and was responsible for the deaths of at least twenty-three men. Robbery and pillaging were also part of his criminal repertoire. An altogether bad hombre, Queho had to be stopped. But how? No one knew the area around the canyon better than Queho. Each time lawmen came searching for him, they left empty-handed. After committing his crimes, Queho would take refuge in the rocks and caves. He could always wait them out.

Eventually the lawmen who had pursued Queho gave up on ever finding him. They grew old, then died. And still no sign of Queho. Numerous stories went around the city: Queho was long gone, and living far from the area. He walked the streets of Las Vegas, big as you please. His ghost hovered over the canyon, taunting all those who had ever chased him. It seemed that there was a different tale for every day of the week. Then one day in 1940 the mystery was solved.

On a warm February morning three prospectors were working along a steep cliff high above the Colorado River in the Black Rock Canyon. One of the men discovered a low stone wall near a spot some two thousand feet above the river. This would make the perfect hideout, he thought, as he gazed down into the canyon far below. From this vantage point, a person could see in all directions. He called to his friends, who came running. As the men explored further they discovered a small cave with a trip wire running across it. Why on earth, they wondered, would someone set up a crude alarm system at the cave's entrance?

Their prospecting forgotten, the men crept inside the cave where they found the mummified remains of a man. Huddled up in a fetal position, the man had apparently died in a lot of pain. The dead man's personal effects were scattered around the cave. These items included several pairs of eyeglasses and shoes, an assortment of weapons, and the badge of a night watchman from the Gold Bug Mine.

Had the infamous Queho been found at last? The debate was on. The Las Vegas chief of police and the coroner went to the cave for a look-see. The coroner conducted an inquest on the spot; his verdict was that natural causes, and not a rattler, had caused Queho's doom. They were so certain of the corpse's identity that the chief of police would later admit to kicking it in the behind—something he had waited long years to do.

That was only the beginning of a long line of indignities the mummified Queho would endure. The remains were put on display in the Clark County courthouse where the ghoulishly curious could come and take a peek. When interest waned, the dead Queho was taken to a local mortuary; three years later he was still there. The Las Vegas chief of police agreed to pay the mortuary its fees and gave the mummified Queho to the Las Vegas Elks, who put him on display during the big Helldorado festivities.

In the 1950s someone stole Queho's bones and scattered them in Bonanza Wash. Hopefully, Queho, or what was left of him, would stay there forever. It wasn't to be.

Somehow Queho's bones were rediscovered and sold to a local Pahrump man for one hundred dollars. At long last the old renegade's remains were finally buried. Rest in peace, Queho. Let's hope your postmortem traveling days are past.

It's a long way from Queho's gravesite in the Pahrump Valley to Eldorado Canyon. Still you have to wonder if that shadow moving across the rocks doesn't belong to the ghostly Queho.

The Lost Breyfogle Mine

Okay, so there are the slots, blackjack, and roulette, but there are other ways to get rich in Las Vegas. All you have to do is locate the Lost Breyfogle Mine. How hard can that be? They say that the mine is out there in the Southern Nevada desert somewhere. Grab your metal detector and start your search out among the sagebrush, the Joshua trees, and the sand. There is no telling how many treasures and lost mines you might discover out in the desert.

None are like the legendary Lost Breyfogle with its gold nuggets as big as a man's fist. And one of these days, somebody is going to find it. Along the way they might run into the ghostly Charles Breyfogle.

In 1863 prospector Charles Breyfogle set out south of Austin with his pack horses, his dreams, and his supplies. After spending several days in the desert, Breyfogle happened upon gold beyond his wildest imaginings. Luck had finally shone down on him. He could not have known how fickle that luck would be as he greedily loaded his canvas sacks full of gold nuggets. Congratulating himself on his find, Breyfogle daydreamed about how he would spend all his wealth: the places he would go, the things he would buy.

Days passed. Breyfogle got so caught up with his find and his plans that he ignored his horses, which wandered off into the desert never to be seen again. Unfortunately the prospector's supplies were packed on the animals. When he realized what had happened, Breyfogle tried desperately to find the horses. Eventually he ended up lost himself. Resolving to memorize the mine's location, he began walking back toward Austin. Without water, the prospector became disoriented and hopelessly lost. He was dying of thirst when two drifters happened upon him. If not for their kindness, Breyfogle would have died out there in the desert.

In this regard, luck was shining down. The strangers nursed him back to health and helped him make his way back to Austin. After showing off a nugget and sharing his tale of a rich vein, Breyfogle convinced several men to grubstake a return trip to the mine.

Weeks later all hopes were dashed; the mine could not be found. In spite of one failure after one, Breyfogle could always spin a good enough yarn to convince someone to help in his quest. But each new venture met with failure. Eventually, even he had to give up the search as a lost cause; the Breyfogle was gone forever.

Over the years hundreds of people have combed the desert looking for the lost Breyfogle Mine. Every one of them has come away disappointed and empty-handed. But this doesn't stop others from trying. Theories as to the mine's location abound. It may be somewhere just south of Tonopah, in the Armagosa Valley, outside of Pahrump, or in a top-secret area of the gunnery range at Nellis Air Force Base.

Another theory is that the Lost Breyfogle was worked under another name long ago, and is all played out. Treasure hunters aren't buying it. The Lost Breyfogle Mine is out there in the Southern Nevada desert just waiting for some lucky soul to stumble upon it. With all-terrain vehicles, bottled water, cell phones, metal detectors, and global positioning systems, they are better equipped than Charles Breyfogle ever dreamed of being.

Perhaps someone will get lucky one of these days and happen upon the mine. But keep in mind that whoever discovers the Lost Breyfogle may also encounter the ghostly Charles Breyfogle, who, some believe, watches over his lost mine. If you should be out in the desert some day and see something shimmering in the sunlight, think twice before you stoop to pick it up. Old Charles Breyfogle was so heartbroken at not being able to locate his mine, he may not take kindly to someone hauling away his gold nuggets. But hey, all you have to do is convince the ghostly prospector that gold is worthless in the hereafter.

Put those nuggets down, Breyfogle, and go toward the light. Please.

Chapter 6

Bureaucracy, Red Tape, and Specters

Bureaucratic red tape; once you get wrapped up in it, it's difficult to free yourself: Fill out this form, take a number, and wait. And wait . . . and wait . . . and wait.

Nellis Air Force Base

In 1940 the U.S. Army Corps of Engineers began its search for a suitable location for a flexible aerial gunnery school. Several areas of Nevada, Arizona, and Utah were up for consideration.

In the end the location near Las Vegas was chosen for its nearly perfect flying weather and its desert terrain. Besides that, the dollar per acre price, for the public domain land, couldn't be beat. Originally named Las Vegas Air Force Base, the name was later changed to Nellis in honor of William Harrell Nellis who was killed in action during World War II.

Located about eight miles from downtown Las Vegas, Nellis covers more than two million acres and is known as the Home of the Fighter Pilot. It is also known as harboring some secrets.

Deep within the confines of Nellis Air Force Base is the mysterious Area 51, also known as Groom Lake. No one, other than authorized personnel, is permitted access. No one! The compound is impenetrable; any place off site that might afford a view belongs to the federal government and is also off limits. Warning signs are clearly posted, and armed guards reconnoiter the entire area. Trespassers will always be arrested. No excuses, no exceptions.

Why all this secrecy, you ask. UFOs, captive aliens, and secret experiments are rumored to be the reason for the government's diligence in keeping people out.

These aren't the only strange goings-on here at Nellis Air Force Base. According to some, the base is haunted. Over the years, several witnesses have reported seeing a ghostly gray man wandering in certain hangars, specifically Jet Engine Intermediate Maintenance Facility Building 858. He is believed to be an unfortunate airman who lost his life in a jet crash decades ago. In yet another hangar unexplained footsteps, laughter, and moaning can occasionally be heard.

At least one house at Nellis may also be haunted.

> We were living in a house on the base at Nellis. There was this presence in the house that didn't like me or my children. When my husband was home, there were never any problems. But when he had to be away, the thing did everything it could to scare us half to death.
>
> The windows would rattle and shake, the lights would go off and would not turn on, water in the kitchen would start running, and the toilets would flush and fill up all night long. It was the scariest thing that has ever happened to me. One night I got so mad I yelled out, "Stop it!" and it did stop for awhile. Then there was this horrible god-awful stench. I searched every inch of the house and never did find what caused it.
>
> When my husband returned, everything went back to normal. I told him about the ghost and how it bothered me and the kids, but he just laughed it off. I even tried to get this group of ghost hunters I knew to come and see what they could, but they wouldn't come unless I had "official permission." It was such a relief when we were finally able to move away.

Nellis Tragedy

They were young, and married, and the parents of a baby girl. He worked as a police officer at Nellis Air Force Base. She was a housewife. Her days were spent cleaning and cooking and taking care of their baby. It was the early

1950s when this lifestyle was the accepted norm.

Like all young couples they enjoyed an occasional night out. With Helldorado in full force, they hired a babysitter and joined the fun-loving crowd downtown. Hours later they returned home, paid the babysitter, and prepared for bed.

Awakened by the sound of her parents' laughter, the toddler started to whimper. Her mother cradled her lovingly and rocked her back to sleep. The baby's father sat directly across from them loading his gun. He was a police officer. He knew about burglars, robbers, and killers. His family would always be protected.

Then, without warning, the gun discharged. A bullet struck the baby in the forehead, just missing its mother. Frozen in horror, the young man could do nothing but stare. One long, loud, agonizing scream escaped from his wife.

Alarmed by the noise, neighbors came running. An ambulance was called, and the fatally wounded child was rushed to a nearby hospital. Out of his mind with grief, the young man crawled under the bed and refused to come out until police threatened him with tear gas. The child's death was found to be a tragic accident, but the baby's father would never be the same.

Saucers over Sin City

Area 51 and Groom Lake are the unknown of Nellis. Reports of weird aircraft and other strange goings on there are the norm. Of the sightings reported in the Southern Nevada desert, none are stranger than that witnessed by three tourists en route to Las Vegas decades ago.

As their car sped down the lonely highway, the sun dropped into the horizon and the sky turned from deep rich purple to pitch black. A sliver of moon crested the hills, but they hardly noticed as they joked about the bundle each hoped to win in what they affectionately referred to as "Lost Wages."

They rode in companionable silence a while, then the subject of dinner came up. While they discussed the specialties of different casino coffee shops, a bright light flashed in the distance, and something caught their eyes. All three gazed in amazement at what they would later describe as a shiny smooth flying saucer. The object seemed to be hovering near Las Vegas.

"What in the world?" the driver asked his passengers.

"Looks like some sort of flying saucer!"

"Maybe it's a new sign they're putting up in Las Vegas."

"No. It's some sort of . . ." He hesitated. "It's a flying saucer all right!"

And then as quickly as it had appeared, the dome-shaped craft vanished.

Had they seen a ghostly craft from another galaxy, time travelers from our own planet, or just some weird desert mirage? The three witnesses didn't know what it was, but they knew it was not like anything they had ever seen before.

Within a few years there would be more reports of strange craft and weird lights in the skies over Las Vegas. One witness would describe something like a giant string of white lights hovering over Sunrise Mountain. Doubters would cast suspicious eyes at those who told of seeing unusual phenomena; nonetheless, the reports continued.

Crash

It was April 21, 1958. Spring had come to the desert. There wasn't a cloud in the sky. A student pilot and his instructor took off from Nellis Air Force Base in an F-100F fighter jet. In Los Angeles, 275 miles away, forty-seven people boarded a DC-7 commercial airliner bound for New York. Within the hour all would be dead . . .

An elderly couple working in their garden heard the sound of a terrible explosion. Looking toward the desert, they saw the gray white puff of smoke. A local casino owner was out in his private plane for an early morning flight over the Las Vegas Valley. Suddenly a mayday call rattled on his radio. He looked out and saw pieces of wreckage fluttering to earth.

Twelve miles south of Las Vegas the fighter jet had collided with the airliner; the ensuing wreckage was strewn over several miles. Sixteen years earlier actress Carole Lombard had lost her life in a plane crash in the same vicinity.

As the bodies were recovered, they were taken by military ambulance to a makeshift mortuary at the old Las Vegas racetrack. Las Vegas was smaller then. There were only three funeral homes in town. As one newspaper of the day reported, "Morticians from all three funeral homes appeared with cases of embalming fluid."

Within the year new flight patterns and regulations would be in place for Nellis Air Force Base jets and all other aircraft, private and commercial. Never again would such a tragedy be allowed to occur.

Clark County Recorder's Office

From the moment you see it, the Clark County Government Center is a pleasant surprise. In this city noted for its neon and outrageous glitz, the government center stands out as unique and tastefully designed. The county's business is conducted here in the main building, a sleek terra-cotta modern with dark glass windows. The smaller pyramid-shaped building serves as a cafeteria and meeting room.

Everything here is surrounded by cacti, rock, and other desert-hardy plants. Close your eyes. This could be anywhere in the Desert Southwest. But gasp, it's Las Vegas, and the design is subtle and as new as tomorrow. The whole shebang is not much older than a decade, and already haunted. Can you really blame a ghost for choosing such digs?

The ghost of an elderly man haunts the Clark County Recorder's Office on the second floor of the main building. Several people who work in the office have seen, or felt, the old gent's presence. Not content to spend all his time in the office, the specter gets around. He divides his time between the office, the rotunda, and the stairs.

Those in the know claim the ghost is Mr. Clayton, Clark County's first elected recorder, who has come to lodge in this up-to-the-minute building. Clayton, so the story goes, met his death one night on the railroad tracks that ran nearby. To this day, just how the oldster met his demise is a much-debated topic. Was he the victim of foul play? Did he stumble and fall in front of the train, or did he just get so tired of this world that he decided to move on to the next? Whatever the reason, Clayton was dead. And so he was buried in an unmarked grave and forgotten.

When everyone moved into the new building, he came along, taking up residence in the county recorder's office. He is not malicious, and no one is frightened of him. Still, proprieties must be upheld. A new headstone and grave were donated, and Clayton's grave was rededicated. A nice gesture, indeed, but apparently the ghost still makes an occasional appearance at the government center building.

Clark County Coroner's Office

We are all a bit curious as to the inner workings of the coroner's office. Think not? Then why the popularity of television shows like *Bones,* and *CSI: Las Vegas, Miami,* and *New York?*

Extraordinary things do occur at the coroner's little corner of the universe. In this place mysteries are explained, and law enforcement personnel are aided in the solving of crimes. Hopefully this is so.

Unless a person dies of some catastrophic illness in a hospital bed, chances are good he or she will make a personal appearance at the coroner's. Rich, famous, and dead, or broke, unknown, and dead, it makes no difference. Hundreds of bodies arrive at the Clark County Coroner's Office each year. Most of them are autopsied and sent on their way. Occasionally something bizarre happens. The following incident is an example.

While working on a large gasoline tank, a man removed his oxygen mask, complained of feeling sick, and then stumbled and fell forty feet to his death in the tank. It was an hour before the body could be retrieved and taken to the coroner's office. There it was left overnight in the refrigerator, a matter of routine. Next day as the autopsy began; noxious fumes arose from the body.

The coroner's office was evacuated and closed for the day, until a hazardous material team could come in and make certain there was no longer any danger to the living.

When it was safe to do so, everyone in the building returned to work, and it was business as usual.

Police Work

Police officers see it all: the good, the bad, and the bizarre. Occasionally officers of the law have a brush with the supernatural, no matter how tenuous. Are ghosts to blame for those events that occur without explanation? Is there really such a thing as coincidence?

"I Don't Want to Hear It"

When the police pulled him over, the young AWOL serviceman was driving erratically. Making matters worse, he was behind the wheel of a stolen car. For these infractions of the law, he was promptly arrested and taken to jail.

Police work in the 1950s was not high tech. Without the help of databases and computers it took a few days for the police to discover that the owner of the stolen car was in California. But he wasn't coming to Las Vegas to claim his vehicle. He was dead of massive head injuries and had been for a week; his body had lain in his small home undetected.

Las Vegas police were curious. Before he was extradited, the soldier was questioned. Why? Why kill someone just to steal a car? His reply was swift. It was not so much the car he wanted, as it was silence. It was all this talk of ghosts. He explained that he had just gotten sick and tired of the victim's incessant talk of ghosts and disembodied spirits.

"Somebody's Watching Me"

The distraught man went to the police department with

a serious complaint. For some unknown reason someone was following him everywhere he went, and he wanted it stopped. After careful questioning, the police determined that no one was following the man. Perhaps he could find some answers at the mental health facility.

No! One way or another he was determined to stop the person who was tagging along behind him. He found that way one morning on the highway between Boulder City and Las Vegas. As the truck approached, he waved madly to the driver. Before the driver could react, he dove under the truck, killing himself and putting an end to his torment.

Ghost in Jail

Why are some places more haunted than others? Every paranormal researcher seems to have his or her favorite theory. There seem to be as many theories about hauntings as there are paranormal researchers. One thing most of them agree on is the part that strong emotion plays in a haunting. Nothing holds a ghost in one place like anger, love, horror, hatred, and fear. Is it any wonder that jails and prisons are haunted? There are stories of ghosts who reside in jails and prisons all across the United States. Alcatraz, in San Francisco Bay, and the old jail in Charleston, South Carolina, are two examples of places where ghosts remain incarcerated into the hereafter.

It was in the 1950s, long before the City of Las Vegas Police Department merged with the Clark County Sheriff's Department to form the Las Vegas Metropolitan Police Department (called the Metro). It was Thanksgiving Day. Throughout the city, families gathered before their televisions and their roast turkey dinners.

Casinos are 24/7 operations. Those who earn their living in the industry either reschedule the holidays for their days off, or eat the festive meal at work. So it was on this Thanksgiving in the fifties; casino employees hurriedly ate their turkey in employee cafeterias and rushed back onto the floor. The gambling public must be served, holiday or not.

Thunderbird circa 1950s (note the names on the billboard)

His coins gobbled up by the slot machines, the old man stopped at the coffee shop and ate his special Turkey dinner with all the trimmings. He was just another guy who had followed his dream to Las Vegas. Things didn't pan out. And now he was alone. Holidays were always the toughest. Here it was Thanksgiving, and he had no one and nothing to be thankful for. No one would care if he lived or died. That settled it. Without family or friends, the elderly man took his own life. Whatever his reasons for leaving this world, he didn't do so without a will.

And what a strange will it was. The oldster left all his worldly possessions, paltry as they were, to the Las Vegas police chief, who had no idea why he was the beneficiary. Another mystery for city officials was the explicit funeral instructions the deceased had also left in the chief's care.

While city fathers tried to untangle it all, the old man's body reposed at the city morgue. Back in the city jail, inmates complained of strange occurrences going on there. Suddenly there were unexplained cold drafts and mumbling voices. All the weird goings-on led some to believe the jail just might be haunted; even though it wasn't the horrible old 1910 jail, but the new jail that was less than ten years old.

Chapter 7

Boulder City Haunts

Boulder Dam/Hoover Dam:
A Dam by Any Other Name

No matter how many times historians try to dispel them, the rumors keep surfacing. These stories of bodies buried in Hoover Dam have been circulating for years. In these gruesome tales men who toppled to their deaths were covered over by tons of steel and concrete. Don't believe a word of it. None of the men who died working on Boulder Dam are buried within its massive concrete walls.

These tall tales regularly make the rounds. They are only

The roadway over the dam has since been redesigned and rerouted

the stuff of urban legend. But don't think for a minute there aren't any ghosts wandering around Hoover Dam. There are plenty. They are either the men who worked and died here, or those who have committed suicide at the dam. Yeah, it's a long way down. This leap was once a favorite for anyone intent on ending it all. This situation may change with the new highway that bypasses the dam altogether.

When the shift is over, most of us are only too eager to leave our jobs behind. There are of course the truly dedicated, the employees who decide to stay on at their jobs indefinitely. Yes, even after they die. Yikes! There are two of them at the dam. One of the mysterious phantom workers is believed to be a young man who died while working the night shift long ago. This ghostly employee usually appears in hard hat and work clothes, ready to put in his eight hours. He is most often spotted near the elevator or by certain workstations. Another specter appears in one of the dam's powerhouses. He seems to be from the dam's earliest days.

Hoover Dam intake room where numerous ghost sightings have occurred

His lips move as if to speak, but no words come forth. Maybe he is asking, "Is it quitting time yet?"

It was thirteen years from the planning stages to the actual completion of Hoover Dam.

Work on the dam was dangerous; in all, 108 men died on the project. Most of the deaths were attributed to drowning, electrocution, falls, and explosions. There was also the intense heat. During the planning stages little consideration had been given to how hot it could get in the Southern Nevada desert. Temperatures soared well over the hundred-degree mark and stayed there. Anyone who wasn't used to the heat suffered, some more than others. Thirteen men succumbed to the heat.

And while we are on the subject of dam deaths, consider this: the strangest coincidence connected with the dam are the deaths of Patrick Tierney and his father, J. G. On the morning of December 20, 1922, J. G. Tierney was surveying the dam's proposed location on the Colorado River. When he fell from the barge and drowned, Tierney became the first man to die on the project. Exactly thirteen years later, to the day, his son Patrick Tierney became the last man to die on the Hoover Dam project when he fell to his death from an intake tower on December 20, 1935.

A Dam Site Closer to Town

In the Las Vegas area, Hoover Dam is a favorite site for suicides. This may be because the dam is close to the city. Unfortunately, suicide is a fact of life. The taking of one's own life is a quick way out of problems, real and imagined. It's an escape, if you will, an escape that leaves behind broken hearts and unanswered questions.

Contrary to what you may think, Nevada does not lead the nation in suicides. Neither does Las Vegas. And yet, this city, sparkling with so much promise, is the final destination for some of those wishing to end it all. Perhaps it is the city's allure. After all, there is no place on earth quite like Las Vegas.

Hoover Dam a long way down

Obviously hotel/casino spokespersons are reluctant to talk about the suicides that have occurred on their property.

In the past ten years three people have gone to the top of the Stratosphere and dived headlong onto the street below. At the Luxor a man decided to jump from the eighth floor down into the casino. A distraught young woman leaped to her death from the ninth floor of a casino parking garage. Others have shot, poisoned, or hanged themselves out of this world. Where there's a will, there's a way.

A recent divorcée, saddened with the direction of her life, drove to the dam and jumped into oblivion. When a young couple flew across the country to vacation in Las Vegas, neither of them realized what fate had in store for them. Two days after their arrival, they had a violent argument in their Strip hotel room.

He was so enraged that he beat his girlfriend nearly to death, and then finished the job by strangling her. When he realized what he had done, the man sped to Hoover Dam and jumped to his death.

Howling on Hoover Dam

Not all of Hoover Dam's ghosts are of the human variety. A bronze plaque near the parking area commemorates the little black sheperd whose ghost has been seen numerous times as he scampers across the roadway and disappears into thin air. He was just a mutt. But the men took the puppy to their hearts after his mother abandoned him. The little dog quickly became the beloved mascot of those who worked on the Boulder Dam project.

On their way to work each morning, several of the men would stop to give him a friendly pat on the head. Times were tough, but his food and water dishes were always full. In appreciation, the dog, who was able to sense when a man was in danger, warned supervisors whenever an accident had occurred and someone's life was in jeopardy.

Unfortunately, none of his human friends possessed the

same sixth sense. Tragedy struck one morning when a truck accidentally backed over him while he slept. There was nothing they could do for him. The heartbroken men scooped up his broken little body and buried him only a few yards from where he was born.

Today absolutely no pets are allowed on the dam. So if a dog should run out in front of you, remember that he is only the ghostly dog of the dam.

Boulder City

Don't come to Boulder City with a cup full of coins and expecting to spend some time parked at a liberal slot machine. You're not going to roll the dice, shoot craps, or play blackjack here either. Boulder City has the distinction of being the only city in Nevada where gambling is not permitted. That's right, folks; there are no casinos here. So put away your lucky rabbit's foot. When the yen to beat the house comes, remember that Las Vegas is only twenty miles away.

Boulder City began in 1928 with the Bureau of Reclamation's decision to build Boulder Dam. All those workers necessary to turn the plan into reality would need a place to live. So a community had to be created. The city of Denver's landscape architect Saco Rienk DeBoer was signed on to design the city, and work began.

But there were concerns. Given its close proximity to Las Vegas the new city could easily fall prey to the same vices to which the rest of Nevada had succumbed. To assuage these worries, the Bureau of Reclamation put the newly created city under its control. That way there would be no alcohol sales, no prostitution, and no gambling. It was the city's strict moral code that sent single workers hotfooting it down the Boulder Highway toward Las Vegas with all its gambling, booze, and women.

Boulder City would be under the Bureau of Reclamation's control for the next thirty years. It wouldn't be until 1960 that it was officially incorporated. The city has relaxed its policy on liquor sales, but gambling is prohibited by a city charter. And what of that other vice, prostitution? Well yes, it is legal in many parts of Nevada, but not here in Clark County.

With all the action and attention centered at the building of Boulder Dam, Boulder City became the first city in Clark County (sorry, Vegas) to have its own airport. During construction of the dam, the city would remain more popular than Las Vegas. Everyone, from the rich and famous, to the just plain curious, flocked to Boulder City just to catch a glimpse of the dam's construction. And when they got here, they needed a place to stay.

Boulder Dam Hotel

Construction began on the Boulder Dam Hotel in September 1933. Two months later, it opened with a gala celebration. In an article announcing the hotel's opening, the December 15, 1933, edition of the *Las Vegas Evening Review-Journal* stated, "The hotel compares in beauty with any famous hotels along the coast and has the advantage of smallness."

The rich and the famous have slept at the hotel. Movie stars Robert Taylor, Ronald Coleman, Shirley Temple, Harold Lloyd, Bette Davis, and Boris Karloff were guests. Karloff waited out his six-week divorce residency at the hotel; once it was obtained, he and the new missus were married. Off with the old, on with the new. A favorite Boulder City story has Shirley Temple and parents staying at the hotel and visiting the local school. When one pupil asked the curly-haired child actress, "What makes you any different from me?" the dimpled darling replied, "I have money."

Smart lass.

Sportsmen, who came for the fishing and other water activities at nearby Lake Mead, stayed at the hotel. Movie stars like Fred MacMurray, who came for the fishing, and billionaire Howard Hughes, who came for the flying, were among them.

On the afternoon of May 17, 1943, reclusive Howard Hughes and a crew of four was testing his Sikorsky S-43 on the waters of Lake Mead. The amphibious aircraft skittered across the lake, lifted up, and crashed back down into the water. Hughes sustained several injuries, including cracked ribs, and one of his crew members was killed. The plane sank into the two-hundred-foot depths of the manmade lake, from which it was later retrieved.

Hughes would spend the next several months recuperating at the hotel. He was kind to the help, but standoffish. Eccentric even then, he insisted that his room be cleaned in a certain way each day.

The hotel was closed down for quite a while, but it is once again accepting guests. Some of them report encounters of the ghostly sort. A woman who visited the hotel recently told the following:

> My friend and I had just had lunch, and so wanted to repair our lipstick. While I was waiting outside the ladies' restroom for her, I happened to glance at the piano in the main room. All of a sudden I heard the clearest piano music. I was trying to make out the tune when my friend came out. "What is that tune?" I asked her.
>
> She shook her head. "I don't hear anything."
>
> "Listen," I said. "I think . . . Yes, it's 'My Funny Valentine.'"
>
> She looked at me oddly. "I don't hear anyone playing the piano."
>
> It was the strangest thing. I know what I heard.

Among the spirits thought to haunt this hotel are an elderly gentleman and a young murder victim. They have been seen throughout the building. Orbs and other anomalies often show up in photographs taken inside the hotel. During a recent paranormal investigation of the hotel, some people reported hearing the sound of crying in the hallways.

Author Dennis McBride brought a well-known psychic to

the hotel in 1980. After a two-hour investigation, she had channeled several spirits, an event that McBride covers in his fascinating book *Midnight on Arizona Street: The Secret Life of the Boulder Dam Hotel.*

Boulder City/Hoover Dam Museum

Located in the Boulder Dam Hotel, the Boulder City/ Hoover Dam Museum is a must-see if you want to learn more about the history of Hoover Dam. The museum presents an extensive overview of the Boulder Canyon Project from its inception to the opening of the dam. Oral histories, photographs, maps, and interactive displays tell the story of the building of Boulder Dam, from the human aspect; the toll it took on the workers and their families; and how it changed their lives forever.

Years ago author and Boulder City historian Dennis McBride had an encounter with a ghost at the museum. McBride, who was a collections specialist at the museum, was working alone one evening in the building when he happened to look up and see a man standing in the doorway. He described the man as dark, mustached, and visible only from the waist up. McBride did not sense any malevolence, only that the spirit was curious about what he was doing.

The ghost could be anybody. He may have been a man who lost his life on the dam, and followed some of his personal belongings to the museum. Or he could be a ghost just passing through. We may never know his identity, or why he chose to come to the museum, but it's a safe bet he isn't the only spirit residing in a museum.

Boulder Theater

Back in 1931 when it was built, the Boulder Theater was the only building in Boulder City with air-conditioning. Imagine the business the theater did on a sweltering summer night. Imagine it especially since no gambling establishments or bars were permitted in town.

On New Year's Eve 1934 the theater was the site of the gala world premier of the movie *The Silver Streak.* Several Hollywood luminaries came to Boulder City especially for the event. Shot in and around Boulder City and the dam, the movie featured several not so famous actors and actresses. It would never be a big hit. Tonight that didn't matter. All eyes were on the screen at the Boulder Theater as the house lights dimmed. In a few hours they would ring in a new year. The theater was ablaze with the glitter of diamonds, the rustle of silk, and the softness of fur. The aroma of perfume, expensive and exotic, filled the air.

Las Vegas was still the dusty little cowpoke town where anything went. It would be a decade before the stars seriously played and partied there.

It would be longer still before thousands of people would crowd onto The Strip to witness the old year melt into the new, in a spectacular pyrotechnic display. Someday Las Vegas would be the entertainment capital of the world, but not on this night. As long as construction on the dam continued, Boulder City would be favored by stars. This was New Year's Eve 1934, and the Boulder Theater was dazzling.

But time moves on. The 1990s saw a new era of larger, high-tech, multi-screen theaters, with surround sound and slick snack bars. The Boulder Theater couldn't compete, and was forced to close. It was then purchased by Desi Arnaz Jr. and his wife Amy who founded the non-profit children's ballet company, the Boulder City Ballet Company (BCBC.) Today the theater is listed on the National Register of Historic Places. And although films have not been shown at the four-hundred-seat theater in more than a decade, it is the home of the BCBC and remains a state-of-the-art live theater venue, a place of family entertainment. And as is the case with most theaters, it is said to have its resident ghosts.

Recently, a lighting director was working alone in the theater. Engrossed in the task at hand, he happened to look up and see the faint figure of a man slowly walking toward him. An eerie silence fell on the room. As the ghostly figure came nearer, the lighting director realized what he was watching was not of this earth.

He could flee in fear, or he could stand his ground. He chose to stand his ground, and said calmly. "Tell you what, I'll leave you alone if you leave me alone."

As if in agreement the ghost vanished.

"Thank you," the lighting director said, and went back to his work.

A tap teacher had a more harrowing experience. He was rehearsing alone in the theater one night, when he was suddenly surrounded by an icy chill.

Thinking that a door or a window had been left opened, he looked for the source of the cold breeze. Everything was shut tight. Shivering, he told himself there had to be an explanation. Maybe a vent was open, he thought, looking toward the ceiling, hopefully. At that moment something, or someone, startled him with a gentle tap on the shoulder. He nearly jumped from the stage; it was enough to convince him that the theater was haunted. From that day forward, he refused to be alone in the building after dark.

There are numerous reasons why theaters are haunted. Actors craving the spotlight in the hereafter, audiences enjoying a play, the myriad of emotions played out in the building, are but a few. Sudden death is yet another.

Records show that a man died of a heart attack in the early 1940s while watching a movie at the theater. Some believe this unfortunate man is the source of the Boulder Theater's haunting. And it well could be.

Pass the popcorn, please.

Boulder City Pet Cemetery

The Boulder City Pet Cemetery is difficult to find, especially if you are looking for an expanse of well-manicured lawn, ornate iron gates, or graceful walls. Think disarray, desert sand, and sagebrush. A large lot that is dotted with every sort of remembrance and handmade marker, this is the Boulder City Pet Cemetery. It may not be an official cemetery, but over the past five decades hundreds of beloved Las Vegas pets have been buried here. Like all cemeteries, it is a place for honoring and remembering.

Our pets deserve nothing less. They are our treasured companions. They enrich our lives immeasurably, and ask so little in return. Their deaths leave us with empty places in our hearts. Some researchers believe it is our pain at their passing that keeps them anchored to our world. This could be the reason for the sightings of ghostly inhabitants wandering the cemetery after dark. More than one person has seen the large golden lab wandering aimlessly through the cemetery, only to vanish into thin air. Talking about felines now, a pet parent shared the following story.

My Frankie's death happened so suddenly. He'd always been such a healthy cat, never been sick a day in his life, and then one day, he refused to eat, and didn't want to do anything but sleep. I thought he probably had a cold or something when I took him to the vet. But it was far worse. I wasn't prepared for the news the vet had for me.

"I'm afraid Frankie isn't long for this world," the doctor told me sadly.

Within the week Frankie was dead. I missed him so much. They talk about an aching heart; I knew how that felt. I was still trying to get used to being without him. Frankie had only been dead a few weeks, and I was still driving out to the pet cemetery after work to visit his grave. I stood there watching the sun go down and in spite of myself I smiled at the memory of him as a kitten and how he had run around about the condominium, so full of life. He was always into something.

Off in the distance, I noticed a large white cat heading straight for me.

"Nice kitty," I called absently. The cat hurried to me and happily brushed against my legs. I knelt down to pet the cat and was stunned when my hand touched nothing but air. I have another cat now, but I still go the cemetery once in a while . . . I've not seen the white cat again.

Others have also seen this ghostly white cat that disappears into thin air.

My folks had recently bought a condo in Boulder City and invited us for dinner. We were on our way there when I looked out and saw this big white cat wandering in the desert. "Stop the car!" I yelled to my husband. "Stop right now!" There was no way I was going to let that cat stay out there and get eaten by coyotes.

He pulled the car over to the side of the road, and we jumped out. "You see him over there?" I asked my husband as I slowly walked toward the cat.

"You're going to scare him off," my husband cautioned.

I know cats. The best way to approach them is to let them know you're interested in them, without being aggressive about it.

"Here, kitty, kitty, kitty," I called to him, and he came running.

When he was close enough I reached down to pick him up, but there was nothing. I tell you that cat just vanished right there in front of us. I don't know who was more shocked, my husband or me. We decided not to tell the folks about it. My mom would be worried that it was some sort of omen, and my dad would think we had lost our minds. Every time we drive past there now I look for him. But I've never seen him since that day.

Remember this story if you are driving down Boulder Highway at night and happen to see a ghostly feline scampering across the sagebrush at the Boulder City Pet Cemetery.

Elderly Ghost on Boulder Highway

There is little doubt that many roadways are haunted. Every year thousands of motorists perish in wrecks. A recurring theme in the research of ghosts is *sudden unexpected death.* Imagine, one moment you are alive, and the next you are confused and disoriented. No one is listening to a word you have to say. Everyone is ignoring you. It's almost as if you don't exist. This may be an explanation for ghostly activity. In that case, a haunting may be nothing more than a ghost's attempts at communicating with the living.

Years ago an elderly couple was driving along a lonely stretch of the Boulder Highway outside of Las Vegas. They were headed home. Happily, they agreed that this had been one of their best vacations. They had enjoyed a good run at the slot machines. The wife's coin purse was fuller than it had been when they arrived in Las Vegas the previous week. A great success, their annual vacation to the Desert City had been both fun and profitable. And now they were already engrossed in plans for next year's jaunt. Suddenly their car smashed into something.

Pulling over to the side of the road, the old man got out to see what he had hit. An animal lover, he hated the thought . . . but there it was, a dying cow lay in the middle of the road. There was nothing he could do for the pitiful animal. He couldn't give it anything to ease its suffering or put it out of its misery. As he stood staring down at the cow a large truck came barreling down the highway toward him.

Fear seized the old woman. Frantic that her husband might be killed, she jumped out of the car and waved her arms wildly in warning to the truck. The truck driver tried desperately to brake and avoid the man in the middle of the road. Unfortunately he could not prevent his truck from sliding into the old gentleman, killing him instantly.

Since that tragic event several people have seen the elderly man on the side of the road. Some have slowed down to offer the oldster a ride. He never accepts but merely waves the car on as if to say, "You go on. I'm going to be here a while . . . a very long while."

Chapter 8

Ghosts of Goodsprings

If you stop looking at the bright lights and the round-the-clock action a moment, you will see that Las Vegas is unique in several ways. One of these is its proximity to some very small towns. We are talking towns with populations of four hundred or less. How many major cities do you know of that are surrounded by so many miniscule towns?

Not San Francisco, New York, or Los Angeles, but take a look at Las Vegas and you will notice some tiny cities within a very short driving distance. Time has forgotten many of these towns that were, in their heyday, larger and more important than Las Vegas. Now some of them are closer to ghost town status. Goodsprings is one such town.

Located only forty miles southwest of Las Vegas, Goodsprings is a world apart. In this town of approximately two hundred, there is no neon, no traffic jams, or overcrowding.

It may be hard to believe now, but Goodsprings was once a booming metropolis with more than thirty mines operating in the area.

That was back in 1914 when World War I was raging in Europe. With the war effort, demand for the area's zinc and copper was at an all-time high. As prices of these metals skyrocketed, so did the number of mining operations. It was all good signs for Goodsprings.

Mining brought an influx of money, businesses, and people to town. But like so many other Nevada boomtowns, the end came as quickly as its beginning. When the war was over, the mining boom was finished. Without jobs, most of the residents of Goodsprings had no choice but to pack up and leave.

Unless some movie company is doing filming in town, Goodsprings is relatively quiet these days. That is except for the Saturday night jukebox over at the Pioneer Saloon. Proof of early-day mining activity is a scattering of old cabins and rusted-out mining implements; these are about the only sign of the boom that once took place here.

Goodsprings Cemetery

The Spanish Flu pandemic lasted from 1918 to 1919. In that time it would kill millions of people worldwide. Not all of them were old or infirm. Many of the pandemic's victims were young, healthy adults like Goodsprings businessman George Arthur Fayle. On the morning of December 9, 1918, Fayle had been ill with the dreaded influenza for a week. In the afternoon, Fayle seemed to rally. Family and friends were overjoyed; it looked as if he was about to make a full recovery. Unfortunately, they were wrong. George Fayle would be dead by nightfall. He was thirty-seven years old.

Three days later, mourners gathered in the dining room of the Fayle Hotel for the funeral. Afterward, according to his wishes, Fayle was buried near a little knoll in the Goodsprings Cemetery. He rests there today beside his wife Jean, for whom the nearby city of Jean is named. Take a stroll among the desert sand and sagebrush and you will find the graves of other early-day Nevada pioneers. You might also encounter a ghost or two.

The lonely lady ghost may be one of those you meet. She floats silently across the old markers and is said to be a long-ago resident of Goodsprings who died under mysterious circumstances. With each telling, the story changes; the lady was murdered, she died in a speeding car crash, or she took her own life. All we know is the lady ghost is dead; we may never know how she got that way.

Over the years, the lonely lady ghost has been seen by more than one ghost-hunting group.

Is the Goodsprings Cemetery haunted, or isn't it? While paranormal researchers are quick to point out that not every cemetery is haunted, several of them are. And if you believe the stories, Goodsprings Cemetery is inhabited by three specters. At least that's what some ghost hunters who have spent time in the cemetery claim.

A couple of ghostly children are said to roam through the cemetery after dark. Unlike some ghostly graveyard residents, the two tykes seem content to be there. Ghost hunters come and go. Some are drawn by the ghost sightings and stories of others. Most just want to investigate the paranormal away from the bright lights of Las Vegas. During investigations enough photographs and EVP have been collected to convince ghost hunters the place truly is haunted.

If you should visit the cemetery, please remember to be respectful of those who rest here.

Goodsprings School

Where there are students, there must be schools, such as they are. The very first school in Goodsprings was a tent. As the town grew, so did the number of students. And students should have something more substantial in which to learn. So a school was built in 1913. Since then, the building has been remodeled several times, but the basic structure, including the old school bell, remains. Listed on the National Register of Historic Places, it is still in use today. This makes it one of the oldest schools in Clark County.

As might be expected, ghosts are rumored to be in residence. The apparition of a long-ago teacher has been seen peering out from one of the schoolroom windows. Perhaps she is watching the three ghostly students who skip merrily on the school grounds only to run into thin air. Or maybe she hears the ghostly children's laughter that some have reportedly heard. Spurred on by the tales of laughter, a group of ghost investigators recently conducted an impromptu EVP session near the school; they didn't capture any discernible laughter.

Campbell Cabin

Rattlesnakes, scorpions, and Joshua trees: this is the Nevada desert. A haunted cabin is in keeping with the region. While most everyone else in Goodsprings is fast asleep, the ghosts of old Campbell Cabin are wreaking havoc. Mysterious lights, sorrowful moans, and foul odors are said to emanate from the old cabin in the wee hours of the morning. The oldest structure in town, the rock cabin was built in 1886 by A. G. Campbell, a wealthy Utah mining promoter who owned several claims in the area. He was also instrumental in the development of Goodsprings as a community, but the town was named after local cattleman Joseph Good.

After residing in the cabin for several years, Campbell moved to a more suitable home. The cabin was vacant for nearly ten years before A. E. Thomas moved in. It could be that A. E. is the ghost who kicks up his heels and makes mischief in the old Campbell Cabin.

Pioneer Saloon

Local businessman George Arthur Fayle, owner of the Fayle Hotel, built the Pioneer Saloon in 1915. At that time Goodsprings was a thriving town. Things may have slowed down for Goodsprings since then, but the saloon, which is the town's only surviving business, remains the locals' favorite hangout. Day or night, the Pioneer Saloon is usually rocking.

Drive up any day of the week, and you are liable to see the parking lot lined with motorcycles. If the place looks familiar, you've probably seen it in a movie. Scenes from the hilarious *Miss Congeniality 2* were filmed here, as were scenes from *Fear and Loathing in Las Vegas.* But you are here for the ghosts. Come on in. Grab a stool. Order up a

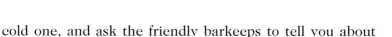

cold one, and ask the friendly barkeeps to tell you about the saloon's ghosts.

No one is shy about ghosts around here. They will gladly fill you in on all the details of how a gambling miner's cheating ways spelled his doom. Paul Coski thought he had everyone fooled. He didn't. When Coski dealt himself a winning card from the bottom of the deck, others noticed. He wasn't as slick as he thought.

On June 26, 1915, at one o'clock in the morning, the day's heat was a memory; a cool breeze wafted through the Pioneer Saloon. In a corner of the saloon six men were quietly playing stud poker. Paul Coski, Joe Armstrong, Roy Blood, Tom Lowe, and F. J. Schroeder were so engrossed in their cards they barely noticed the bartender who hovered nearby. It was Coski's turn to deal. Blood, Armstrong, and Schroeder folded; only Coski and Lowe remained.

"You dealt yourself a card from the bottom," Armstrong told Coski. "You and Tom should split the pot and be done with it."

"He's right, you did," the bartender, who had also been watching, chimed in.

They all agreed. It was late. The pot should be divided and the game ended. Paul Coski took umbrage with the decision. He angrily grabbed for the money. Armstrong leaped up and pushed him back. "There's no call for cheating."

Coski, a powerfully built, former prizefighter tried to jump over the table. The smaller and older Armstrong pulled his gun. Coski grabbed his wrist to disarm him. Armstrong fired, hitting Coski in the hand. Coski lunged for Armstrong, who fired another shot. The bullet hit its target, and Paul Coski fell to the floor dead.

On hearing of the shooting, the sheriff, the district attorney, and the coroner drove out to the Pioneer Saloon. When they arrived hours later, an investigation and inquest were held. Paul Coski had a reputation as being violent and hard to get along with. No one had a good word to say about the cheating miner. Armstrong, on the other hand, was well liked. He had never given anyone a day's trouble.

The ruling was self-defense. Armstrong was exonerated, and Coski's body was wrapped in sheets, placed in a pine box, and buried in the cemetery. Ashes to ashes dust to dust; but the bullet holes remain in the wall of the Pioneer Saloon to this day.

A copy of coroner W. H. Harkins' letter hangs on the wall. It's obvious that the coroner knew what Coski was all about. "He could whip any two men in or around Goodsprings and made a practice of doing the same once in a while when he would get to drinking," he wrote, and then softened the blow with, "When he was sober, he was a gentleman."

It seems that Corski may not be resting in peace. Corroborating the tale of the ghostly miner are the numerous witnesses who have seen the miner's apparition standing at the front door, or sitting at the far end of the bar.

"I sat down next to the old guy and asked what time it was. He ignored me. I asked him again, before I realized I was talking to a ghost," said a patron who encountered the ghostly gambler.

Several of the saloon's customers have rubbed shoulders with its ghosts. A woman who stopped in one evening told the following story:

> The bar was really crowded that night. There was only one seat at the far end, so I took it. Next thing I know this old man is standing next to me. I was fired from my job the day before and wasn't in the mood for any nonsense. So I told him to beat it. He just stood there grinning at me. I called the bartender over and asked her what his story was. She got this little smile on her face and said, "Oh him, don't worry about him; he's our ghost."
>
> I turned back to look at him, but he was gone.

And as many ghost investigators can tell you, the Pioneer Saloon's bewhiskered miner is not camera shy. He has been the subject of several ghost hunting television shows and ghost investigations over the years. Some have produced EVP of gunshots and misty photographs as evidence of the miner's existence. They have all discovered what the people around here already know. The ghost likes it here in the saloon just fine. In that respect he may not be alone. Customers have reported chatting with an elderly gent who slips in and out of the bar unseen. The man was a regular who stopped by the saloon every night. When he died, the habit continued. Look over at that piano. It's not broken. Those keys stay depressed because a certain ghost likes them that way.

Apparently none of the ghosts have any intentions of vacating the premises. Why should they? The Pioneer Saloon is down-home comfy. No big-city chrome and glass here. The Old West-style décor and aura of party-hardy fun are just too much for any self-respecting specter to resist. And besides that, they share their digs with a movie star. Or at least some people believe that Carole Lombard haunts the saloon. Lombard died on nearby Mount Potosi in 1942. In honor of her and her husband Clark Gable, a wall in the poolroom is covered with old black-and-white photographs of the stars, together and separate. Tacked among the photographs are yellowing newspaper pages that tell the tragic story of the movie star's death.

Anyone who is familiar with psychometry may be interested to know that a bit of the wreckage sits atop the saloon's old Franklin stove. Psychometry, for those who are not familiar with it, is the practice of picking up feelings and knowledge simply by touching or being near an object. Go ahead, give it a try. Just don't grab the hot stove there.

Carole Lombard: A Star Dies on Mount Potosi

The beautiful blonde was charming them, and she knew it. Undaunted by the winter chill, she smiled happily. Soon she would be on her way home. Perhaps she was thinking not only of the war effort, but also of her handsome husband who waited for her out in California. "Before I say good-bye to you all . . . come on . . . join me in a big cheer. V for victory," Carole Lombard called to the cheering crowd that gathered around her in downtown Indianapolis.

The patriotic star had been on the road in her home state of Indiana selling war bonds. The campaign was successful; she had raised a record $2,107,513. But now it was time to hurry back to Hollywood and her handsome husband, Clark Gable. If she had been a bit more superstitious, she may not have died up on Mount Potosi that night.

Dreading the long three-day train ride back to California, the actress opted to fly home. Neither her mother nor the friend who was accompanying them wanted to fly back to Hollywood. The friend suffered air sickness. Lombard's mother Elizabeth Peters, a devout numerologist, had other concerns. The date of January 16 portended disaster, she argued. Then too, there were all those threes: three letters in TWA, three people flying on flight number three.

Lombard scoffed. A disagreement ensued. In the end the mother-daughter argument was resolved by the toss of a coin. Lombard was lucky (or was she?); she won the toss. The friend secured their seats on the TWA DC-3 Skylab, and they were on their way home.

Fate would give Carole Lombard two opportunities to avert catastrophe; she ignored the first. In Albuquerque, New Mexico, her second chance came when government officials asked her and her party to give up their seats to servicemen. Lombard was sympathetic to the servicemen's plight. But she refused to budge. She had done her part for the war effort. She was tired and only wanted to get home. And so the plane lifted off into the late afternoon sky. Carole Lombard, her friend, and her mother were the only civilians on board.

The plane landed at the McCarran Airfield (Nellis Air Force Base) in Las Vegas just as darkness settled across the valley. It was almost seven o'clock. After a quick refueling, they were off on the final leg of their journey. A few minutes later, miners working in the area heard an airplane's engines roaring overhead. At the sound of a thunderous explosion, they looked up to see a fireball out near Mount Potosi; flames could be seen for miles. From her nearby ranch, former silent screen star Clara Bow watched the plane burn against the side of the mountain.

There are no definite answers as to what caused the crash. One theory is that the pilot miscalculated and was flying the plane off course. Another story is that the pilot took time to chat with Carole Lombard, leaving the plane in the hands of his less experienced copilot.

When told about his wife's plane crash, Clark Gable rushed to Las Vegas where he spent anxious hours at the El Rancho Vegas, awaiting word of survivors. Friends drove him to Goodsprings, so that he would be closer to the scene. There he stayed at the Fayle Hotel and Pioneer Saloon, near the makeshift operations headquarters in Goodsprings. They say he got tumbledown drunk as the hours passed; cigarette burns on the cherry wood bar are said to be his.

The rescue effort would be extremely difficult. It was the middle of January. Up on the almost eight-thousand-foot mark of Mount Potosi, relentless winter winds whipped across the mountain, bringing heavy snowfall that would hamper rescuers who hiked up the side of the mountain in search of survivors.

Sixteen hours would pass before searchers were able to make their way to the crash site. Once there, they realized that theirs was not to be a rescue mission. All twenty-two people aboard the plane had perished in the crash. Charred and broken bodies were strewn around the wreckage. One man would later say that the snow was red with blood. Ms. Lombard's burned body was discovered under one of the plane's wings. On seeing her tousled blond hair in the snow, searchers were certain they had found the actress's remains. But it would take dental charts flown in from Hollywood to positively identify the blonde comedian.

As the bodies were recovered, they were wrapped in brown army blankets, one by one, and carefully hoisted down the cliff and taken by horse to Goodsprings. There they were placed in waiting Army ambulances and transported to Las Vegas.

Lombard's civilian war effort was not forgotten. President Franklin Delano Roosevelt paid homage to the actress with these words, "She gave unselfishly of time and talent to serve her government in peace and war."

On January 16, the anniversary of the tragic plane crash, an airplane can sometimes be heard roaring across the night sky as it heads out toward Mount Potosi. Look up, and it's gone . . .

According to some longtime Las Vegans, pieces of the wreckage could be seen out on Mount Potosi, glittering in the afternoon sky, for many years afterward. It has been more than sixty years, and rusted parts of the wreckage are still scattered about at the crash site. Also at Mount Potosi there was once a monument dedicated to those who lost their lives in the crash. It read:

> MT. POTOSI, NEVADA
> IN MEMORY
> of the 22 individuals who perished
> on this mountain on January 16 1942,
> in the crash of Transcontinental and
> Western Airlines (TWA) flight 3, including
> Carole Lombard, 15 Army Air Corp pilots,
> a crew of 3, and 3 passengers.

Chapter 9

Lost City, Valley of Fire, Logandale, and Lake Mead

Centuries before Benjamin "Bugsy" Siegel set eyes on Las Vegas this land was lush, green, and watery. It was alive with vibrant flora, fauna, and the sound of creatures now long extinct. Their end would come in a flash. Over time, the world they knew would be swept away, and the once-verdant region would be transformed into the harsh inhospitable desert it is today.

Tourists arriving at McCarran International Airport probably don't realize that ninety miles from the Vegas nightlife and neon are the remains of an ancient civilization and a mystery that has baffled archaeologists since its discovery.

Thousands of years ago the Anasazi lived along the Muddy and Virgin Rivers near present-day Overton. A peaceful people, the Anasazi are categorized into groups.

The first group were the Basketmaker I, so called for their utilitarian use of the baskets that they wove from yucca plants and willows. Their weaponry was primitive and not always accurate. Using an atlatl, or spear thrower, they hunted for deer, bighorn sheep, lizards, and rabbits.

Like the first group, the Basketmaker II cooked and stored their food in woven baskets. Skilled hunters, they developed a much more effective method of hunting game. They used bows and arrows, rather than the crude atlatl.

The final group to inhabit this area was the Puebloans who made their utensils of more practical clay. An industrious people, they raised crops such as corn, cotton, and beans, and were mining turquoise and salt as valuable commodities, hundreds of years before Comstock miners in the northern part of Nevada discovered silver.

And then, as quickly as they had come; the Anasazi vanished, leaving more questions than answers. Archaeologists still don't know why they left the area so abruptly or where they went. Remnants of their civilization, and its secrets, would lay hidden deep beneath the hard dry soil for centuries.

About the time the Declaration of Independence was being signed back East, Spanish missionaries started looking for a route between their missions in Arizona and those in California. They first entered present-day Southern Nevada sometime around 1776. The route they carved out would be known as the Spanish Trail. Fifty years later Antonio Armijo's party of traders was traveling along the trail when scout Rafael Rivera decided to take a shortcut.

Whatever his reasons, Rivera was rewarded with a breathtaking sight. Before him were lush, verdant natural springs that glittered in the scorching sun. Word quickly spread of the welcoming oasis with its cool relief from the hostile desert environment; soon others would find their way to the natural springs. This area would become known as *Las Vegas,* Spanish for "the meadows."

Explorer Jedidiah Smith, who traversed the area of Southern Nevada in 1826, was the first to make reference to the salt caves and other relics of a past civilization located in the region. The Lost City Museum in Overton displays a replica of the following words Smith wrote to William Clark the Superintendent of Indian Affairs, on July 12, 1827.

> The Paiutes have a number of marble pipes, one of which I obtained and sent to you. Although it has been broken since I have had it in my possession; they told me there was a quantity of the same material south of their country. I also obtained a knife of flint, which I send you, but it has likewise been broken by accident.

This early discovery by Jedidiah Smith went almost unnoticed and aroused little curiosity. Two decades later, Captain John C. Fremont would change that with his 1845 expedition of the area.

Of what would later become the location of the city of Las Vegas, Fremont wrote:

> We encamped in the midst of another very large basin, at a camping ground called Las Vegas-a term which the Spaniards use to signify fertile or marshy plains, in contradistinction to llanos, which they apply to dry and sterile plains. Two narrow streams of clear water, four or five feet deep, gush suddenly with a quick current, from two singularly large springs; these, and other waters of the basin, pass out in a gap to the eastward. The taste of the water is good, but rather too warm to be agreeable; the temperature being 71 in the one and 73 in the other. They, however, afford a delightful bathing place.

The way would further be paved for immigrants and merchants to this area when in 1846 Congress printed 20,000 copies of Fremont's report on the expedition and Charles Preuss's map of the area.

Lost City: Pueblo Grande de Nevada

And then in 1924 brothers Fay and John Perkins left their homes in Overton and went out into a remote area of the Southern Nevada Desert to prospect for gold. While on their quest, the men stumbled upon the remnants of a lost civilization. They hurried home to dutifully notify Nevada Governor James Scrugham of their find.

Scrugham, a former state engineer, was quick to realize the importance of the discovery. Nonetheless, the governor was noncommittal until he could see it first hand. After a trip to the site, Scrugham knew this find would claim the world's attention. It was much too important to be left to amateurs. He contacted noted archaeologist M. R.

Harrington of the Heye Foundation in New York, and asked for help in the excavation and study of the area.

As the news of the discovery made its way into newspapers across the globe, worldwide attention focused on Nevada, particularly the southern portion of the state. Digging began in November with cooler weather. His chest swelled with pride, Governor Scrugham informed the news media, "This will jolt some of those smart Easterners, the fellows who say Nevada is so raw and new. They think we have no past, no background or antiquity."

The first excavations yielded a treasure trove for archaeologists to study: buried houses (pueblos), clothing, tools, household items, and skeletons buried beneath the floors or in the walls of the communal houses. In all, forty-six structures were uncovered; the largest of these had more than one hundred rooms.

First estimates put the site at seven thousand years old. After a closer examination the Lost City was believed to date from 1500 to 2000 BC. Nearly six miles square, the site had become officially known as Pueblo Grande de Nevada. It stirred the imagination and intrigued scientists and scholars who came to the desert to see the ancient ruins for themselves. They went about their work, relentlessly salvaging, tagging, and categorizing their finds.

But time was not on the side of those who tirelessly sifted through the ruins. While President Herbert Hoover pondered ways to place the site under the protection of the federal government, other plans were in the works. The Boulder Dam Project that would dam part of the Colorado River, and redirect its flow, was already underway.

With the completion of Hoover Dam, the Colorado River was redirected, and the manmade Lake Mead was formed. As the waters of the lake began to swell, early Nevada towns like St. Thomas were lost forever. So too was the ancient Pueblo Grande, the Lost City. Even so, there are still miles of ruins along the Moapa Valley yet to be excavated and studied.

Petroglyphs at the Lost City Museum in Overton

Lost City Museum

The Lost City Museum in Overton is one of the area's most popular attractions. The museum was built by the National Park Service in 1935 so that the artifacts that had been collected from the Lost City Pueblo Grande de Nevada could be displayed. The museum owns one of the most complete collections of the early Pueblo Indians of the Southwest. Starting with the Desert Culture that lived here 10,000 years ago, and continuing on through the Ancient Basketmaker I, II, and Pueblo cultures, the display features many artifacts and treasures recovered from the Pueblo Grande before it was forever submerged beneath the waters of Lake Mead.

Some claim the ghosts of those who lived here long ago haunt the museum and the grounds surrounding it. The sound of singing and laughter has been reportedly heard on the grounds near the replica adobe pueblos. A man who had visited the museum told the following:

My sister and I were the last people to leave the building that afternoon. It was one of those blustery cold days you don't expect in the desert. When we heard the commotion at one of those pueblos out back, Sis laughed and said, "I bet they didn't plan on a day like this for their festivities."

"I wonder why no one in the museum told us about it," I said, not that I really cared. It was just too cold.

"Let's go see what they're doing," Sis said. And off she went.

We heard them chanting and laughing until we got right up on the thing. Then it was silent. I looked inside, and it was dark as night. "Hello," I called out. But from the look on Sis's face I realized that she knew as well as I did the pueblo was empty. It wasn't the wind or some trick of the imagination. Whatever we heard was real, I can tell you that much.

Moapa Valley High School

There are ghosts, and then there are ghosts. The haunted castles of Merrie Olde England with their four-hundred-year-old ghosts have nothing on the Moapa Valley High School. The school is thought to be haunted by members of the ancient Anasazi civilization who lived in the Moapa Valley region thousands of years ago.

No one knows why their culture vanished; when they went, the Anasazi left everything behind. Eighty years after the discovery of the Lost City (Pueblo Grande de Nevada), Anasazi artifacts are still being found in this area.

During the construction of the Moapa Valley High School, Anasazi relics were disturbed and unearthed. Many paranormal researchers theorize that remodeling, or disturbing, an area can cause a certain amount of unrest among the spirits. Couple this fact with the belief that the school was built in an area of ancient burials, and you may have a cause for the unexplained sightings at the school.

Several tall shadowy men have been reported just outside the building. The specters occasionally follow people around the grounds, and then vanish as quickly as they appeared. Perhaps these ghostly gents are also responsible for the weeping and singing that reportedly comes from the school late at night.

A former student said, "I had heard about the shadow ghosts. But I thought it was just some of the seniors trying to scare other kids. I found out they were real the day I lost a bracelet my granny gave me. After school my best friend and I looked everywhere, but we couldn't find it. We were standing in front of the school getting ready to go home when I felt someone staring at me. I looked over at the side of the building, and there were these three really tall men just sort of standing there. While I was watching, they just dropped down and dissolved. It gave me a really creepy feeling, and I started crying because I was scared they would start following me like people say they do. They didn't reappear, but after that, I knew the shadow ghosts were real."

Valley of Fire

If you're looking for something different to do in the Las Vegas area, drive fifty miles northeast to the Valley of Fire State Park, Nevada's oldest and largest state park. Photographers, historians, and people who just want to be astounded by nature's artwork will find the park, with all its red, purple, and orange sandstone, incredible. Millions of years ago this area was covered by an ancient sea. With geological change, the water receded and the ocean floor rose up, forming the magnificent rock formations we see today in the picturesque Valley of Fire.

Many of these colorful rock formations within the park's boundaries date from 600 million years ago—long before human beings came to the region. Estimates of the first arrival of people here vary from 15,000 years to 4,000 years. Only their artwork remains. Petroglyphs, carved into the rocks by the Native Americans who lived in this region hundreds of years ago, adorn many of the rocks in the park. Don't look for translations; no one has been able to decipher their meanings.

The Valley of Fire is a favorite of film companies. Even if you have never visited it, you have probably seen the brilliant orange-red landscape in commercials and movies, especially those featuring an out-of-this-world Mars-like landscape. It was this very landscape that enabled a long-ago Native American man to hide out from the law. Some believe his restless spirit haunts the region still. Lurking in the rocks and caves, he is like a shadow.

Mouse

Mouse's Tank is a favorite spot of park visitors. Named after Mouse, a Paiute who found himself on the wrong side of the law in the late 1800s, Mouse's Tank is a hidden area inside a rock formation in Petroglyph Canyon. While hiding out from the long arm of the law, the clever Mouse was never thirsty. He slaked his thirst by drinking rainwater that was held in a depression of the rock. When he got hungry enough, Mouse sneaked out of his secret place, came down into the valley, and stole whatever he needed.

There are several different versions of the story of Mouse and the crimes he committed. Thievery and murder top the long list of his offenses. Hunger was his undoing. One July morning he came down out of the Valley of Fire to find food. After stealing from a farmer, Mouse got careless. Anxious to get back to the safety of his hiding place, he didn't realize that an angry posse had picked up his trail and were following him back to the Valley of Fire.

When demanded that he surrender, Mouse pulled his gun and fired wildly. Not finding exactly what they had in mind, the posse opened fire, putting an end to the legend of the renegade who had avoided apprehension for so long out here in the unforgiving desert.

Logandale

Logandale is situated on the north end of Lake Mead. It's a small community approximately fifty miles southeast of Las Vegas, near Overton and the Lost City Museum.

Logandale is especially proud of its museum and cultural center in the old Logandale School. The school was built in 1935, about the same time that Hoover Dam was being completed. It was the first school in Nevada to implement a hot lunch program for its students. The price of the meal was ten cents. Not everyone could pay. But no one went hungry; the children whose families could not afford the dime were fed the same as those who could.

As more families moved into the tiny farming community a larger school was needed. Once it was completed the town found other uses for the old Logandale School; two of which were as a town hall and a funeral parlor.

Old Logandale School

If you're on the trail of history and/or ghosts you might want to stop in at the Old Logandale School Museum; you just might run into one or two here.

The ghost that usually grabs the attention at the Old Logandale School is that of a sandy-haired little boy who is believed to have died near the school long ago. He is mischievous and doesn't mind tapping someone on the shoulder, or turning on the water faucets in the women's bathroom.

A few years ago a woman and her daughter were visiting the school. As they walked down the long hall, they laughed and talked about whether or not the old building had its share of ghosts. The younger woman, who was wearing a floor-length skirt, suddenly jumped. "I just felt a distinct tug on my skirt."

The two women rushed into the office and blurted out, "You'll probably think I am crazy, but just now out in the hall something pulled on my skirt."

"Oh, that was the little boy ghost," said one of the office workers with a smile. "He does that every now and again."

The little boy may not be the only revenant in residence. According to some of those who work in the building, a librarian who worked at the school for many years also visits from time to time. She was meticulous and organized, and probably comes around to make certain that everything is still in order at the old school. Whenever anything is misplaced, she is called upon to help locate it. Invariably, the missing item turns up.

Lake Mead

With Hoover Dam completed, water from the Colorado River began spilling over and filling Lake Mead. Residents of nearby St. Thomas, Callville, and Rioville had already received word that their towns would eventually be covered by the waters of the lake. Valuable lumber and other building material was hauled away from the water's path. The living were safely relocated; then it was time to remove their dead. Residents of St. Thomas worked at a frenzied pace, digging up one gravesite after another in their effort to relocate their cemetery to Overton.

On June 11, 1938, the waters rushed in, and the Pueblo Grande de Nevada, as well as St. Thomas, Callville, and Rioville, were completely submerged beneath a hundred feet of water. When the area is severely drought ridden, Lake Mead recedes, and remnants of long-ago St. Thomas can clearly be seen. This is when a ghostly young lady slowly walks among the ruins of the old water-sodden ghost towns. But there are other ghosts as well.

Surrounded by a richly colored landscape, Lake Mead sparkles sapphire in the hot afternoon sun, belying the many tragedies and deaths that have occurred beneath its surface. Plane crashes, boating accidents, and drownings have claimed the lives of several people since the lake was created. Most of their bodies have been recovered. Some have been lost forever to the lake's murky depths.

Pegleg's Gold Mine

Pegleg Smith's gold mine may also be lost forever beneath the waters of Lake Mead. The lake covers the point where the Colorado River and the Virgin River once converged. Somewhere in this vicinity old Pegleg and a friend discovered nuggets they thought were copper. They were wrong. Years later, during the California Gold Rush, Pegleg happened upon a friend who proudly showed him a bag of gold nuggets. As he stared at the nuggets, Pegleg realized he had made a dreadful mistake on the banks of the Colorado River so long ago.

He would be a wealthy man if he could relocate that mine. Twenty years may have dimmed his memory, but Pegleg felt confident. And he could be very convincing. It didn't take long for him to persuade a group of men to accompany him on his journey back to the area.

And so they set out from California with high hopes. At night the men sat around the campfire and listened while Pegleg regaled them with stories of all those gold nuggets just waiting at the water's edge. He knew what he had stumbled upon all those years ago. If he doubted his ability to relocate the mine, Pegleg was wise enough not to say so. Spurred on by Pegleg's tall tales and their own dreams of striking it rich, the men hurried through the desert.

To avoid the intense desert heat, they had ridden through the night on the last leg of their journey. It was barely daybreak when they arrived at the Colorado and Virgin Rivers. With all that gold waiting, there was no time to rest. The men quickly dismounted, and after Pegleg pointed out likely spots, the search began in earnest. Moods were high with anticipation the first several days. But as each successive day ended with nothing more than Pegleg's assurances that the gold was nearby, the mood changed.

They worked in the scorching sun, and camaraderie gave way to petty disputes as tempers grew shorter. No one wanted to question the veracity of Pegleg's story. But where was all that gold he had boasted about? One by one, the men gave in to defeat, packed up, and left the others to their search. None of them had found so much as a flake of gold. If the mine was here, Pegleg could not remember how to find it. Knowing this was his last chance, the old man tried in vain to recall just where the gold was. His failure meant no one would ever again believe a word Pegleg had to say about finding gold in the desert. He died a broken and bitter man.

But not everyone doubted Pegleg's story. He might have forgotten the exact location of the mine, but that didn't mean the gold wasn't there somewhere. Over the next years, hundreds of men would venture out into the desert and attempt to locate old Pegleg's lost gold mine. No one ever did. And if the mine lies beneath the waters of Lake Mead, as some believe it does, no one ever will.

Ghostly Sightings at Lake Mead

He may have boldly embellished his stories, but never in his wildest dreams could old Pegleg have imagined that one day his favorite spot in the desert, and possibly his lost gold mine, would be covered by a manmade lake that stretches for miles. The largest manmade lake in the United States, Lake Mead was named in honor of Elwood Mead, commissioner of the U.S. Bureau of Reclamation from 1924 to 1936. It is a popular recreational spot for Nevada and Arizona fishermen, boaters, water skiers, and swimmers; each year more than a million tourists visit the lake and the Lake Mead Recreation Area.

Some of these visitors have reported ghostly sightings at various locations on the lake. A ghostly young man who happily runs from the water, only to vanish on the shore, has been reported more than once. Perhaps the lake was a favorite place of his, a place that held many fond memories. It is just as easy to believe that a ghost will return to the location he or she held dear in life as it is to believe they are forever chained to a cemetery or the place of their death.

Another sighting at Lake Mead is that of a man and woman who suddenly appear in the darkness and walk into the water. Fully clothed in garb associated with early-day pioneers, the couple chats amicably and walks into the water unperturbed. Some may attribute this apparition to place memory: not really ghosts or a haunting, but a sighting that occurs repeatedly in a certain location. Think of a scene from your favorite movie played over and over, and you get the idea.

You probably won't give much thought to ghostly matters as sunshine glitters on the lake. Fishing, swimming, boating, and a great tan may be all that is on your mind during the day here at Lake Mead. But on a quiet night, with moonlight glistening across the lake's surface, it's easy enough to believe that . . . yes, this body of water is indeed haunted.

Chapter 10

Entrepreneurial Spirits

Las Vegas is the nation's driest major city. Annual rainfall is less than five inches. The city needs water so badly that plans are underway to start siphoning it from smaller towns in the northern part of the state. All this doesn't matter. So what if there isn't enough water, people keep coming. Who cares if there is nothing in the way of natural resources here, this is Las Vegas! And Las Vegas is it, folks. The be-all and the end-all, yeah! It has always been the kind of city that attracts people with dreams and vision and drive.

Benny Binion and the Horseshoe

In 1946 the time had come for Lester "Benny" Binion to move on. Benny had made a very good living in illegal gambling and other assorted crimes in the Dallas area, but things were getting too hot in Texas. The law was no longer willing to look the other way. And the competition was starting to circle like vultures. Top dog, or not, there was only so much a man could do.

If he could get himself a gambling operation in Nevada, where it was legal, Benny figured he would be well ahead of the game and his competition. Yes, Nevada was the key to his successful future. He crammed a suitcase full of cash, loaded the family into his big black Caddie, and headed for Las Vegas. This was a city where a man could make a buck without someone trying to shut him down, or demanding

The statue that honors former Horseshoe owner, Benny Binion

kickback money. Benny wanted to get in on the action.

During Prohibition Benny made his living as a bootlegger. Eventually he turned his hand to a more lucrative vice, illegal gambling. His rap sheet included two murder charges, which he slid out of on self-defense pleas. But that was back in Texas. And this was Las Vegas where gambling was wide open and legal. Binion wasn't about to let a little thing like his criminal past stand in the way of his plans.

Neither was the Nevada Tax Commission. He was duly licensed, and he and a partner opened the Fremont Club downtown. The partnership soured when Benny decided to raise the betting limits that the house would accept.

The friendship would last a lifetime, but the partners went their separate ways. Binion opened his own place and called it the Horseshoe. The casino would remain in the Binion family for more than forty years. It was the first casino to offer high-stakes betting and poker tournaments and the first to add wall-to-wall carpeting. But what really set it apart was the million-dollar display.

The poor boy from Texas was a clever one. He knew how to reel them in. His million-dollar display—one hundred ten-thousand-dollar bills encased in plastic—did just that. The display was strategically placed at the rear of the casino where customers first had to walk past all those tempting slot machines. Then they could gawk to their heart's content. And just to prove to the folks back home how close they had been to all that money, the Horseshoe offered customers a free photograph of themselves standing next to the display. Say cheese! Along with the average man and woman off the street, came the celebrities of the day, eager for a great photo op. Well over five million such photos were snapped; proving once and for all what a shrewd businessman Lester "Benny" Binion was, even if he couldn't read or write.

After Benny's death, ownership of the Horseshoe fell to Benny's offspring, who gave it a gallant try. But overseeing the day-to-day operation of a casino is not as easy as it looks. Trying to hang on to their heritage they sold Benny's million-dollar display. From then on, it all went downhill. Those superstitious souls in Sin City (and who isn't here?) swear that bad things started happening to the Binions after the family sold off Benny's famous display. Benny would never have agreed to the sale, but he was dead and gone and no longer calling the shots.

The Horseshoe was never on a par with the more glamorous hotel/casinos that line The Strip, nor was it meant to be. It was a working man and woman's place in Glitter Gulch, the older section of town. There was nothing slick or uptown about it. But customers returned again and again. They were treated right at Benny's place. Those who tried to cheat the joint regretted their decision. A longtime Las Vegas rumor has a card cheat being pulled from the Horseshoe, taken into the alley, and beaten to a pulp.

Likewise an employee who tried to steal from the boss found himself in a world of hurt. Flip the cards: Binion treated his good employees like gold. And they in turn were loyal to him; many Las Vegans spent their entire casino careers working for Benny. One employee might even spend eternity haunting the nearby parking garage.

The man was a gambler. His tokes covered the rent and the food, but couldn't begin to repay the loans he was racking up all over town. Eventually, he borrowed from the wrong people. When it came time to pay up, his wallet was as empty as his promises to pay tomorrow. Reneging was not an option on such loans. Neither was it a good idea when all you had for collateral was your life.

Unfortunately he learned his lesson the hard way. He didn't have two quarters to rub together, and told his loan shark so. A few days later he started up his car and was blown into oblivion. Death by dynamite! He perished so suddenly, and so unexpectedly, that he wanders the parking garage, a confused specter, not realizing that he has been dead for decades.

A man says, "I saw this guy and could tell he was some kind of ghost or something. He was walking, but he wasn't. His feet were maybe two, three inches off the ground. He came within a couple yards of me, and wasn't looking at anything in particular. I got in my car and looked back; he was gone."

Las Vegas is a city that admires tenacity and ambition. For all his criminal past, and a two-year stretch in Leavenworth Federal Prison, the city adored Benny Binion, the illiterate cowboy who took the town by storm. Near the old Horseshoe, a bronze statue of Benny, astride his horse, attests to this fact. So did the 19,000 well-wishers who came to the Thomas and Mack Arena to pay homage to him during his eighty-third birthday bash.

Binion is long dead. His beloved Horseshoe is no longer owned and operated by his family. There were too many financial woes. His son Ted died under mysterious circumstances in 1998; his death was at the center of a murder trial that rocked Las Vegas. NBC, CBS, ABC, CNN, and *Court TV* all came running for the titillating details. And there were plenty: illegal drugs, a love triangle, the much younger live-in girlfriend that he had met at a topless bar, and a buried crate full of silver coins. The networks foamed at the mouth. No place airs its dirty laundry better than Sin City.

Forget all that "what happens in Vegas stays in Vegas" stuff. The Binion murder story went 'round the world. In the end the jury found that Ted died as a result of his own bad judgment. He was a heroin addict who combined too many different drugs; an accidental overdose did him in.

Whiskey Pete

Nevadans have always been strong willed. Many of them thumbed their nose at Prohibition. This was a "live and let live" state. If a man, or a woman for that matter, wanted liquor, who was the federal government to step in and say no way? There were so many secret stills, those in the know could always slake their thirst at some little speakeasy.

Out in the Southern Nevada desert it was a little tougher to find a drink. The area was even drier than it is today. Perched on the edge of the Mojave Desert it was mighty rough terrain for federal agents to traverse in search of illegal stills. Most didn't bother.

This brought out the entrepreneurial spirit of Pete McIntyre, a cantankerous old codger who ran a gas station a few miles this side of the California-Nevada state line. While Pete pumped gas, and wiped grime from his customers' windshields, he did a lot of thinking. Over time, he had thought it through carefully. He was a smart man. And a smart man could make himself a fortune if he was to offer travelers something stronger than the sugary soda pop he had in the icebox. He reckoned that no one would care way out here in the middle of nowhere: no one except all those thirsty travelers.

So Pete started selling moonshine. There is no telling where he got his illegal inventory, but word soon got out that he had it. Anyone who wanted a nip could stop, fill up the gas tank, and guzzle the good stuff.

The desert was thirsty, business was good, and Pete prospered. Along the way someone started calling him Whiskey Pete. This might have been for the moonshine he offered, or the fact that Pete liked his whiskey as much as the next man. Either way, the moniker stuck. According to legend, Pete got good and drunk one night and, in a somber mood, asked his pals a favor.

When his time came, he wanted to be buried on his own land, and in an upright position. It was the only way, he figured, that he could keep a good eye on his property. As inebriated as Pete, they agreed to his request. Satisfied that he would spend eternity in an upright position, Pete passed the jug of whiskey and asked one more thing of his buddies.

"Don't forget to put a full bottle of whiskey in the box with me."

Well sure, they agreed. It gets awfully hot in the desert and hades, and who knows, heaven may even have a warm spell now and again. Time passed. Pete fell victim to some dreaded lung disease and died. His amigos were called upon to dig a hole deep enough to keep their promise to Pete. They dug well into the night, and old Pete was buried, not standing exactly, but at a slant. In his withered old hand was a full bottle of whiskey. And there, so the story goes, he rested in peace, for decades.

Even when the property was sold and a large hotel/ casino built upon it. Located in Primm, on the California-Nevada border some thirty-five miles west of Las Vegas, the casino was named Whiskey Pete's in honor of the old curmudgeon. Business at the casino was booming. Before long more space was needed.

The area where Pete slumbered eternally was needed for other purposes. And this being Nevada, his remains were dug up and moved to another location on the property. You might think that this would anger Pete. It hasn't. Nor has it stopped him from playing pranks and enjoying the casino activities. Lights sometimes flip off and on in the offices; items are misplaced; and even though the heat register reads a balmy seventy, it feels like a shivering fifty. It's all Pete's doing.

Old Pete has also been known to do a good deed. If you pull into the lot, and your gas tank is nearly empty, Pete just may fill it up for you. According to the story, the ghostly Pete has been known to point a bony finger at an empty gas tank, thereby filling it up. With the price of gas these days, that is indeed a good deed.

When not roaming the parking lot, the ghostly Pete wanders throughout the casino. He is a people watcher and likes to keep an eye on the gamblers. Some describe him as a grizzled old miner; others say he is just an elderly nondescript man in khakis and short sleeves. He may do his good deed, and enjoy the casino atmosphere, but don't go thinking that he is the social type. He isn't. Not knowing that Pete hails from the hereafter, some people have even tried to strike up a conversation with him, only to be rebuffed. Before anyone can get a really good look at him, he vanishes into nothing—probably out into the parking lot looking for empty gas tanks.

Howard Hughes

If Benjamin "Bugsy" Siegel was the father of Las Vegas, Howard Hughes was the city's knight in shining armor.

Aside from his billion-dollar bankroll, Hughes was the visionary who pointed Sin City in a new direction. That direction would squeeze the mob out of the casinos once and for all. And corporations would reign.

But the billionaire's largess did not come without some mighty long strings. Hughes, after all, was accustomed to getting just what he wanted. And what he wanted was to own as many hotel/casino properties as he could get his hands on. Hughes never exactly explained why this was. But then, he had billions of reasons why he didn't have to explain anything he did.

Hughes had long been a visitor and an admirer of Las Vegas. Like Bugsy Siegel before him, he realized the city's untapped potential and predicted that one day more than a million people would live here. That prediction came to pass years ago.

On a November night in 1966 Hughes finally made his move to Las Vegas. It was in the predawn hours of the day before Thanksgiving when his train pulled into town. Nothing here would ever be the same.

He and his entourage were driven to the Desert Inn. The smell of money was in the air. And the red carpet was rolled out. Hughes and staff were promptly given the best the hotel had to offer, the ninth floor penthouse suites. While Hughes and his minions lived the highlife on the ninth floor, the weeks turned into months, and management started to worry. And as any casino employee can tell you, it's not good when management worries.

Everyone knew that the penthouses were for the exclusive use of high rollers who didn't mind dropping big bucks on the gaming floor. All the cajoling, all the begging, and all the pleading was in vain; nothing worked. Howard Hughes et al. refused to budge. Management made an executive decision.

To hell with him and his ridiculous demands for banana nut ice cream. After months of sweating out where those high rollers would stay, management decreed that the whole Hughes kit and caboodle be evicted. The bottom line needed to be watched, and the high rollers needed those perks. Either that or they would take their money elsewhere. The thought of all that money going into the coffers of another casino was enough to make management cry real tears, or to break out in a cold sweat.

Didn't they get it? Hughes liked the Desert Inn, and wasn't about to leave his penthouse suite. How much? Just name your price. In true billionaire fashion, he pulled out his checkbook and bought the Desert Inn. The mob was out, and the corporation was in.

And then the supply of banana nut ice cream dwindled. It was Hughes's favorite flavor. How dare Baskin-Robbins discontinue it? Mr. Hughes was to be kept happy at all costs. That was the mantra his employees lived by. A phone call was placed to Baskin-Robbins headquarters in Los Angeles. Certainly the ice cream could still be had, but only in increments of four-hundred-plus gallons. Money was no object. The ice cream was ordered and delivered.

There was a sigh of relief; the barrels were in the freezer. About that time the eccentric Hughes decided he preferred French vanilla; from here on out it was the only flavor ice cream he wanted to eat. Free ice cream. Step right up. For months afterward Desert Inn customers were treated to free ice cream (banana nut naturally).

Hughes was an insomniac. The spinning sign across the street at the Silver Slipper didn't help. A gigantic high heel spinning round and round, each turn sent flashes of light sparkling through Hughes's window. He was a billionaire. He could afford to be as eccentric as he wanted to be. If not for the annoying spinning silver slipper would Hughes have bought up half of Las Vegas? Probably so; at any rate this was the beginning of his purchasing one casino after another. Now that he was owner of the Silver Slipper, the sign had to come down. At last he would get some sleep.

But nothing comes without a price. Howard Hughes realized this fact better than most. Then came the hoops Hughes had to jump through. According to Nevada law

The spinning silver slipper that drove Howard Hughes to insomnia

no one can own a casino unless he or she is licensed by the Nevada Gaming Commission. This meant a personal appearance by Hughes before the regulatory board where his life would be laid bare and carefully scrutinized. He would also be called upon to answer question after question about his finances.

The very thought of it threw the eccentric Hughes into a tailspin. Rules are made for those without enough money to break them. Hughes promised a substantial donation to the University of Nevada-Las Vegas medical school, he had no criminal history, and he was much too busy to be bothered with making a personal appearance. So he sent his minions instead. And wouldn't you know it! Howard Hughes got his license. Later he would renege on the med school donation promise.

With his gaming license, there was no stopping him. In quick succession he bought what he wanted: the Sands, the Castaways, and the Landmark. In doing so, he changed the way Las Vegas casinos did business. The knee breakers were out, and the bean counters were in. Welcome to corporate America.

Ten years later, he was gone. As quickly as he had come to Las Vegas, Hughes sold his casino interests and moved on. He died in 1976 aboard an airplane headed from Mexico to Texas. Shortly after his death, maids working in the Desert Inn penthouse suites reported seeing his apparition; he was even spotted on the casino floor a couple of times. The ghostly Howard was not the emaciated, long-nailed, stringy-haired wretch he was at death, but the young, virile, robust Howard, who had wined and dined Jane Russell and other circa 1940s lovelies all over Hollywood.

And the world moved on. By 2001 the Desert Inn was a few years beyond forty. Old by Vegas standards, it was all set to come down. The place would have to make room for the new Wynn Las Vegas. And rumors started flying. As with many other Nevada properties, there were tunnels beneath the old D.I. Perhaps they were dug with nothing more sinister in mind than deliveries and repairs. On hearing a Las Vegas story that went around town shortly before the Desert Inn was demolished, ghost hunters licked their chops in eager anticipation. Word on the street was that the ghostly Howard Hughes had left the penthouse suite and was residing in the Desert Inn tunnels.

Well, why not? If Elvis, Redd Foxx, and Liberace were sticking around Las Vegas, why couldn't Howard Hughes. Now just suppose that the billionaire's spirit was really wandering around down there. Can you imagine how quickly the paranormal world would be set on its ear if someone were to capture the voice of the long-dead Howard? "Got any banana nut ice cream?"

Who wanted to be the first ghost hunter to make contact? Everyone in town did! Before any of them could pull out their dowsing rods, EMF meters, cameras, recorders, and other ghost-hunting paraphernalia, the place was demolished. Sorry, Howard. Surely you can understand the need to continually develop Sin City's valuable real estate.

Soup, Salad, and a Ghost

Hold the meat and potatoes. Not all Las Vegas entrepreneurs are in the casinos. Some are in the restaurants. You may be wondering why any entrepreneur would go into the restaurant business when everyone says it is so tough. Competition is stiff, and the public's idea of what constitutes a good meal is always changing. Not to worry: Las Vegas restaurateurs can keep up. This is a city of first-class dining; many of the world's top chefs create their magic in upscale kitchens all across the valley. Take a moment to look over the menu while you consider this story that, according to those who told it, took place in a small restaurant several years ago.

The couple discovered the elegant little restaurant by chance. They had spent a grueling afternoon looking at new cars, comparing sticker prices and options. When hunger struck, it hit hard.

New cars were forgotten for the time being as they went in search of a place to eat. Fast food was fine for their workday fare, but it was the weekend, and they wanted something nicer, something with soup and salad, flickering candles, soft music, and a wine list that offered more than red or white.

They found it at the restaurant that quickly became their favorite. By the time they purchased their new car, they had fallen into a comfortable routine of starting each weekend with dinner here. Their dining pleasure was further enhanced by the capable service of their favorite waiter, Enrique.

Always jovial, he regaled them with the latest kitchen gossip while seeing to their every need. True or not, the tidbits he told were lighthearted and entertaining. But Enrique was first and foremost a top-notch waiter; he remembered their favorite dishes, and knew what specials, or new delicacies, to suggest. After a meal was concluded, he invariably presented the dessert tray with a flourish and the words, "What is life without our sweet little sins?"

Occasionally they agreed and hungrily dove into thick slabs of New York-style cheesecake topped with glazed raspberries; most of the time they declined with a chuckle. "Well, we won't be sinning tonight."

In time their schedules changed, and the Friday night ritual of dining at the restaurant abruptly ended. Months went by. When they again found themselves sharing a Friday night off they decided to celebrate by dining at their favorite restaurant.

The moment they walked in, a somber mood struck them. No one in the place seemed to be smiling. The maitre d' who usually seated them so cheerfully was sullen. He led them to a corner table and skulked away silently. They glanced at their menus, then scanned the room for Enrique, who was nowhere in sight.

"Chef must be in a very sour mood tonight," she said absently.

"Either that, or someone lost a bundle at the tables," he smiled, remembering Enrique's tale of those on the staff who liked to bet big at blackjack.

"Oh look, there's Enrique now," she said, waving to the waiter who stood across the room from them.

"I don't think he saw you," her husband told her.

At that moment Enrique approached their table. Without smiling or acknowledging them, the waiter slowly turned and walked in the other direction. He stopped, absently wiped a table with his snow-white towel, and then headed toward the kitchen.

"Now I know what a rebuff is," the husband laughed. "I wonder what his problem is."

"I don't know, maybe a love affair gone awry," she surmised jokingly.

Soon another waiter was at the table. He filled their water goblets and said, "Good evening, my name is Philippe, and I will be your server tonight. May I suggest the veal piccata or—"

She didn't let him finish his well-rehearsed spiel. "Aren't we sitting in Enrique's section?"

Philippe nodded somberly that it was so.

"We just saw him headed toward the kitchen. Will you kindly ask him to come out here and wait on us?"

"I am so sorry, madam, but—"

The wife interrupted again. "What is wrong? Everyone, even Enrique, seems to be in a bad mood tonight!"

The waiter motioned to the maitre d', who came running.

"They saw Enrique going into the kitchen," Philippe told him.

The maitre d' sternly looked first at the wife then at the husband. "I am afraid that is quite impossible!"

"Well, just go in the kitchen and—"

"Madam does not understand," the maitre d' interrupted.

"I understand that Enrique will not come out here and wait—"

The maitre d' lost his patience. "Enrique was killed in a car accident yesterday in Seattle," he said sadly.

They shivered as cold chills rushed through them. They knew what they had seen. And what they had seen was Enrique, but there was no point in pursuing the argument. After apologies all around, they decided against dinner, and went home to ponder how strange life can be.

Bibliography

Burbank, Jeff. *Las Vegas Babylon: True Tales of Glitter, Glamour, and Greed.* New York: M. Evans, 2005.

Coakley, Deidre, Hank Greenspun, and Gary C. Gerard. *The Day the MGM Grand Hotel Burned.* Secaucus, N.J.: Lyle Stuart, 1982.

Dobie, J. Frank. "The Lost Breyfogle Mine." *True West Magazine* 4, no. 5 (1957).

Hauck, Dennis William. *Haunted Places: The National Directory.* New York: Penguin, 2002.

Hopkins, A. D., and K. J. Evans. *The First 100: Portraits of the Men and Women Who Shaped Las Vegas.* Las Vegas: Huntington, 2000.

Jennings, Dean. *We Only Kill Each Other: The Life and Bad Times of Bugsy Siegel.* New York: Fawcett, 1968.

Kelley, Kitty. *His Way: An Unauthorized Biography of Frank Sinatra.* New York: Bantam, 1987.

Land, Barbara, Myrick Land, and Guy Lewis Rocha. *A Short History of Las Vegas,* 2nd ed. Reno: University of Nevada Press, 2004.

Laytner, Ron. *The True Story of Howard Hughes in Las Vegas.* Charleston, S.C.: Book Surge, 2007.

Levy, Shawn. *Rat Pack Confidential: Frank, Dean, Sammy, Peter, Joey and the Last Great Show Biz Party.* New York: Doubleday, 1999.

McBride, Dennis. *Midnight on Arizona Street: The Secret Life of the Boulder Dam Hotel.* Boulder City, N.V.: Boulder City/Hoover Dam Museum, 1993.

McCracken, Robert D. *Las Vegas: The Great American Playground.* Reno: University of Nevada Press, 1996.

McDonald, Douglas. *Nevada: Lost Mines and Buried Treasure.* Reno: Stanley Paher, 1981.

McKenney, J. Wilson. *On the Trail of Pegleg Smith's Lost Gold: Legend and Fact Combined to Provide Fresh Clues to the Location of Pegleg Smith's Famous Lost Mine.* Palm Desert, Calif.: Desert Press, 1957.

Moehring, Eugene P. *Resort City in the Sunbelt: Las Vegas 1930-1970.* Reno: University of Nevada Press, 1989.

Newton, Wayne, and Maurice Dick. *Once Before I Go.* New York: Avon, 1991.

Oberding, Janice. *Haunted Nevada,* 2nd ed. Reno: Thunder Mountain, 2003.

Paher, Stanley W. *Las Vegas As It Began, As It Grew.* Reno: Nevada Publications, 1971.

Reid, Ed, and Ovid Demaris. *The Green Felt Jungle.* Cutchogue, N.Y.: Buccaneer Books, 1963.

Renay, Liz. *My First 2000 Men.* Fort Lee, N.J.: Barricade Books, 1992.

Roemer, William F., Jr. *The Enforcer: Spilotro—The Chicago Mob's Man over Las Vegas.* New York: Ivy Books, 1995.

Rothman, Hal. *Neon Metropolis: How Las Vegas Started the Twenty-first Century.* New York: Routledge, 2002.

Scheid, Jeff, and John L. Smith. *Quicksilver: The Ted Binion Murder Case.* Las Vegas: Huntington, 2001.

Scott, Cathy. *The Killing of Tupac Shakur,* 2nd ed. Las Vegas: Huntington, 2002.

Smith, John L. *Sharks in the Desert: The Founding Fathers and Current Kings of Las Vegas.* Fort Lee, N.J.: Barricade Books, 2005.

Summers, Anthony. *Goddess: The Secret Lives of Marilyn Monroe.* London: Orion, 2000.

Thomas, Bo. *Liberace: The True Story.* New York: St. Martin's Press, 1988.

Thorson, Scott. *Behind the Candelabra: My Life with Liberace.* New York: Dutton, 1988.

Wilkerson, W. R., III. *The Man Who Invented Las Vegas.* Bellingham, Wash.: Ciro's Books, 2000.